HOW TO LAND A BETTER JOB

HOW TO LAND A BETTER JOB

Catherine S. Lott
Oscar C. Lott

Printed on recyclable paper

VGM Career Horizons
a division of *NTC Publishing Group*
Lincolnwood, Illinois USA

Library of Congress Cataloging-in-Publication Data

Lott, Catherine S.
   How to land a better job / Catherine S. Lott, Oscar C. Lott.
      p.   cm.
   Includes bibliographical references.
   ISBN 0-8442-4174-1
      1. Vocational guidance—United States.   2. Job hunting—United
States.   I. Lott, Oscar C.   II. Title.
HF5382.5.U5L64   1994
650.14—dc20   93-46211
                                                            CIP

Published by VGM Career Horizons, a division of NTC Publishing Group
4255 West Touhy Avenue
Lincolnwood (Chicago), Illinois 60646-1975, U.S.A.

4 5 6 7 8 9 0 VP 9 8 7 6 5 4 3 2 1

Contents

**How to Get Leads and Appointments:
The Private Sector   24**

Going After a Government Job   40

It Begins Here

This book offers the authors' 50 years of combined experience in all phases of hiring and placing job applicants. And more. Not just jobs. But good jobs, "positions," careers!

What Is a Better Job?   What does "land a better job" mean? It means that if you don't have a job now, if you apply the advice and methods offered here, you'll get a better job than you otherwise would have.

If you already have a job, you will land a better job. Maybe it will be better because it pays more. Maybe it will be a rung on a career ladder leading upward. Maybe it will be better because you'll have a shorter commute, or you will like the boss and coworkers more than you do now.

Whatever your reason for wanting to land a better job,

studying and acting on the advice and techniques offered on these pages will help you get what it is you're after.

The authors have spent more than 50 years as personnel directors, employment managers, and personnel consultants. In their long and varied work experiences, they have hired people; they have assisted people in getting good jobs; they have obtained good jobs themselves. The essence of successful planning and follow-through to locate and win better jobs is presented here.

It is written emphasizing practical things that matter most. The suggestions and advice offered will mean the most to those who have had little or no experience in searching out and landing a fine job, but they can also be immensely valuable to anyone who has experienced too little success in getting and keeping good jobs.

You will find that it contains important "inside information" on how employment managers, interviewers, and bosses screen and select applicants and promote employees in both private organizations and government civil service and merit systems.

Here are some of the things you will learn more about:

- How to present yourself most favorably on paper

- How to beat your competitors through performing outstandingly in your interviews

- How to minimize the negative effects of unfavorable references, of having been a job-hopper, or of having a police record

- How to get transferred or promoted to a better job right where you are working

But learning more about these matters will be of no value unless you use what you learn.

When you finish the book, set it aside and say to yourself: "Okay! I'm going to do it, and I'll start now, today!"

First—Be The Best That You Can Be

1

This book covers all important aspects of getting a better job. These aspects begin with honestly and thoroughly analyzing yourself.

You no doubt are well aware of your good points and your qualifications. You can list your qualifications for your resume and can mention your good points in your interviews.

The First Step: An Honest, Thorough Self-Appraisal

Honestly and thoroughly take stock of any personal deficiencies or weaknesses that may hurt your chances in interviews or in job performance. Doing so will give you the basis for working on your personal faults. You can then become a more ideal candidate and employee, by improving your education, appearance, personality, or anything else that may stand in your way.

What can you add or enhance?

The goal is to add to your "paper" qualifications and enhance your personal attributes so that you'll be a far more saleable applicant.

In doing your self-analysis, be very sure you don't miss any of the following points. If you admit that you're weak and need improvement in any of them, you'll be on your way to becoming a more perfect candidate than if you simply offer yourself on an "as is" basis.

Write down each of the critically important points that follow. After each, jot down how you think you stack up and what you will do to become a stronger competitor for the kinds of better jobs that you want to land!

Appearance
Pretty or handsome and what employers prize

You need not be pretty or handsome in order to land a good job, a better job. Careful grooming, however, is a must. Hair, nails, make-up, and personal cleanliness are a lot more important than you may think. The authors of this book, over many years, have seen quite a few otherwise excellent candidates lose out due to poor or careless grooming.

If you're a young person, you probably like and enjoy wearing the dress styles that are popular with teens and very young adults. Let's assume that you do, and that you don't agree with the older generations who see youngsters' dress styles as weird and wacky.

Be conservative in your attire. When with your friends, you have every right to do as they do, look as they like to look. But have the good sense to dress to fit in with the more mature generations who make virtually all the hiring decisions!

On the use of cosmetics, a man must be *very* conservative, whereas the wise woman should consult with cosmetics experts and cosmetologists, specialists who are concerned with improving skin, hair, and nails.

Look healthy, speak with confidence. Your objective is to be as youthful looking as is appropriate for your age. That means an emphasis on looking extra healthy. A good cosmetics expert will teach you to use make-up with restraint. Avoid the "painted doll" result that detracts from the natural good looks of mature women.

Obesity is another matter. Many employers will conclude that really fat applicants are weak-willed and lazy people. Both men and women pay a severe penalty in competing on the job market if they are overweight. They look older than their years, and interviewers have concerns about the applicants' health as well as how their appearance will affect the organization's image. With women, extra pounds plus lack of physical conditioning can add many years to their chronological age. If possible, stay trim. Or get trim and then stay that way.

Analyze your bodily appearance honestly. If you have blemishes that you feel are unpleasant for others to view and make you feel uncomfortable, pay a visit to a specialist and rid yourself of the problem.

Education   *If you have only a B.A., go for more.*   Except for highly specialized fields, such as engineering or science and medicine, most degree majors are broad enough to help the applicant do a fine job in many diverse fields. However those with only bachelor's degrees in such subjects as social studies, psychology, music, teaching, history, anthropology, political science, and so forth, face limitations in regard to the better jobs in those fields. A master's degree in those fields may help, but a doctorate is needed to open doors to the best opportunities.

That statement is not meant to discourage you from going on to earn an advanced degree. To do so means considerable sacrifice for most people, but if you can possibly go on for advanced studies, by all means do so.

A great many people are seriously handicapped in competing for the better jobs because they failed to get more education or training of the right kind after finishing high school. This applies not only to those who jumped into the first job offered to them after high school. It also includes those who went to college and spent years and money majoring in a subject that was not right for them.

It may not have been right because good jobs in the field are scarce or do not pay well. Those with undergraduate degrees in fields such as history, economics, literature, art, and drama, for example, usually run into this problem. Also, after getting their degree, many simply decide they really don't want to work in those fields.

If you don't have some college credits, get some.   If you have no college or other advanced training, start getting some. Even a few courses will give you an edge when applying for a good job. If you did get a college degree but your major is of little real value in the job market, the amount of time and money that will be needed to solve your problem may be a lot less than you think.

Your college credits or degrees

Degree requirements at virtually all institutions of higher learning include for all majors a substantial number of general subject matter courses, in addition to those relating to the student's major. Thus, many courses will not have to be repeated in switching majors. Further, if it is not practical for you to return to the college where you were awarded the degree, most institutions will give you credits for a significant number of courses completed at another accredited college.

For example, many people with liberal arts degrees who can't get a good job based on those credentials can benefit substantially by switching to a teaching major. Teaching jobs are paying better every year, and those with advanced degrees earn very good money, have excellent benefits and job security, and enjoy the many other benefits of being a teacher.

Again, it is extremely important for you to take at least a few college courses or enroll in a vocational education or commercial training program if you are going to compete successfully for the better jobs. It is not a good idea to let much time pass with the obstacle of a weak education standing in your way. If having the time to attend classes is the problem, good home-study programs cover a great many educational and skill areas. If money is a problem and you have a job, see if your employer provides tuition reimbursement. Most vocational schools and virtually all community colleges have financial assistance available.

Sticking with a program

When you embark on a program to strengthen a weak education, you may be starting on a long journey, particularly if you take on an ambitious program involving months or years of night classes.

Divide your plan into small steps. Then reward yourself as you complete each step. Take a weekend trip. Go out to a fancy restaurant. Doing something out of the ordinary will reinforce your determination to achieve your next step. Share your plans and progress with your family and friends. That will also help you when you might otherwise get discouraged and want to give up.

Even if you have to keep a job, or borrow, do it. It will pay you.   You may need to keep the old, dull job for income as you take your new training in the evening hours. Perhaps you may need to borrow money. Nevertheless, if you have been bored, dissatisfied, and at a dead end in your present field of work, go for it. If you are weary of being turned down for jobs partly because your education is weak, go get more education.

College, of course, is not the only road to prepare for one of the better-paying jobs in your community. Vocational training schools, computer schools, secretarial schools, and organizations that offer courses in hairstyling, travel agency work, truck driving, and construction equipment operation can lead to just the type of very good job that will give you happiness and success. A typing course helps many people, because keyboard skills are valuable in most office work.

Even a little extra education or training provides evidence to employers that you are special. It demonstrates that you are ambitious and determined.

Be sure to bring your extra education to the attention of prospective employers. Most application forms are poorly designed to bring out the specifics of courses that applicants have completed.

In summary, if you are miserable doing some type of work that you have been trapped in because of a weak education, pay the price and get whatever it is that you want out of your future years.

Other Problems
Arrests and convictions

If you have never been arrested and convicted of a crime of some seriousness, keep it that way. Most police records are public records and are open and available to organizations that have a legitimate need to know. If you have such a record, see Chapter 5 for some suggestions on dealing with it.

Protect your credit rating

Companies that take care in hiring will usually ask for a credit report on you, and that will reflect your reputation for paying your debts in a timely manner. Why do employers care if you pay your bills promptly or not? Why do they make it their business to take a look at your credit record before they hire you? Because many feel that when people borrow or buy on credit, they are making a promise to pay. If they fail to pay or fall seriously behind, the lending institutions or merchants report their delinquencies or failures to the local credit bureau. Larger employers, particularly, are members of the bureau and can get your file information simply by phoning. On the basis of a bad credit record, many employers will conclude that you do not keep your promises, are irresponsible, or untrustworthy.

Credit bureaus can have information about you that is inaccurate. You have the right to go and examine your file and see that incorrect information is corrected. But stay out of heavy debt, and pay your bills on time. It can keep you from losing out on good jobs that you would otherwise get.

References

Expect employers to check your references. Your employment history is not just what you put down on your resume or application. It is also the reputation that you have built with your employers, past and present. Many employers now are doing a more thorough job of background checking on likely applicants' attitudes, behavior, and performance with previous employers. They talk in detail with those individuals who have been responsible for directly supervising the work of applicants who are about to be hired, and they can check on them in other ways.

You build a valuable reputation with employers in many ways, big and small. For example:

- You arrive on time and work hard when you get to the job.

- You get along well with the other employees, customers, or the public.

- You are easy to supervise and are not given to moodiness, pouting, or argumentativeness.

- You do your work quickly, accurately, and reliably.

- You rarely lose time from work, even in very bad weather.

- You offer to do more than the minimum required.

- You take criticism seriously but in good spirit.

- You show good initiative—the ability to do the right thing at the right time without having to be told.

If you've been discharged from a job for cause, try not to list the person who did the firing as a reference. When asked for a reference, try to list a person from that job you feel will speak well of you. If an associate there will help, you might get by.

Otherwise, pay a visit to the person who is hurting your job chances, and make a plea to him or her to at least mention some of your good points because of the hardships you're experiencing. It may help; it often does.

Age

Is your age a problem?   If you're a mature adult, meaning more than 30 years of age, you're by no means "old," but that doesn't mean you'll never be turned down for a job because you're older than the employer prefers. Naturally, you'll never be given that as the reason you were not hired for the job. That is because laws prohibit discrimination in hiring based on age.

So people can fail to get jobs even when they are in their thirties and forties. When people are in their fifties, the problem intensifies. The age barrier can be worse for senior citizens.

Don't your many years of experience give you an advantage?   Doesn't experience count for something? Sure, but only up to a point. Ten years of secretarial experience is simply not worth twice more than five years. Also, as years on the job accumulate, so do periodic and special pay raises. Those with more experience want more money, but those with less experience come cheaper. That means a lot to many employers. Some people doing hiring associate being young with being smart. Those involved in hiring often use the phrase "bright young people."

If you're somewhat mature, you will be competing at times with younger applicants. If you are middle-aged or beyond, man or woman, stay especially fit and trim.

Look younger, feel younger, stay younger.   If you are a man, never mind that your wife says your graying hair makes you look distinguished. Use one of the many preparations available to darken it, doing the same to your moustache or beard. Keep your hair conservatively but youthfully styled. If you are nearing baldness, get a good hairpiece. Good ones are expensive, but if properly fitted and maintained, they are virtually undetectable, even close-up. If friends tease you about it, take the teasing in stride, and they will soon stop.

Lying about age

Socially, you may want to lie about your age. But in employment situations, it is a definite mistake. In the first place, it doesn't help significantly to knock off a year or two. So you are 36 and you put down 34. You have lied for no justifiable reason. How about the big lie? You are 36 and you tell them you are 29. Very likely a prospective employer will take a close look at you and realize you are lying about your age.

Awkward situations often arise when people lie about their age. If you've lied about your age, you must not show your driver's license. Also, your employer will have to report your earnings, Social Security payments, and other data by your name, Social Security number, and date of birth. The chances are good that your lie will come back to embarrass you and might even delay your retirement.

The midlife crisis

Of all the career crises that happen to people, the midlife unemployed crisis is one of the most traumatic. This crisis occurs when people who are middle-aged lose good jobs. Typically, they have worked for many years for the same organization and have reached a high level of earnings and enjoy a commensurately high life-style. Then the bomb is dropped. The company goes out of business, shuts down the plant or office, sells out to another company, or eliminates many jobs. With varying expressions of commiseration and perhaps some termination money, a middle-aged person is suddenly without a job.

If this has happened to you and you find that getting back onto some organization's payroll at a level commensurate with your worth and need is proving to be extremely difficult, don't get discouraged. Help is available. The subject is too complex for a full treatment here. However, a number of good books on the subject are available at most of the larger public libraries and bookstores. They cover the psychological aspects of handling such crises, family supportiveness, financial management, career field changes, opening a small business, and the names and addresses of organizations that specialize in helping with these situations.

The senior citizen　　People, of course, become old at different ages. Most people look forward to living without a salaried job when they become eligible for a retirement income. Others are not satisfied with an idle life or have a pension that they find to be inadequate, so they want to continue to be employed. Many military personnel are able to retire as young as 40 or even a bit earlier and want a second career. Women are sometimes widowed in their later years. Those left with meager incomes often want to find a job in order to make ends meet.

The most severe problems are faced by those ranging in age from perhaps 50 to 75 or more who really need jobs in order to earn money.

If that is your situation, don't say in interviews that you "just want to keep busy." Everyone knows numerous organizations begging for volunteers that can easily soak up whatever extra time and energy you may have.

Those who already have marketable qualifications, such as solid academic degrees, trade or office skills, and a prior record of work experience, are fortunate; although, due to age, getting one of the better jobs still can be quite difficult.

It is the ones who are thrown into the job market with little or no easily employable knowledge or skill who represent the core of the older and perhaps chronically unemployed.

The information and advice provided in Chapter 2 can be of immense value to nearly everyone who is having difficulty landing a good job. This especially applies to those who have very serious problems, obstacles that continually stand in the way of reaching their goals.

Virtually everyone's problems can be solved.　Those who are in the senior-citizen age bracket and who are faced with one or more of the obstacles covered in this chapter so far often have another hurdle to clear. They may have health problems or physical infirmities that rule out a great many types of jobs. However, while a few may in fact simply be unemployable, virtually everyone's problems can be solved with the right combination of professional assistance, self-help, and some willingness to adjust goals.

If you are in this category, in addition to acknowledging and working to overcome any of the obstacles previously discussed in this chapter, confront your health and vigor limitations. This does not mean just thinking about these things. It means seeing your doctor, getting a thorough checkup, and getting as many facts as you can about what you can and cannot handle.

Adjusting goals   If you are older and have been having a lot of trouble getting the kind of job you want, you may have to adjust your goals in order to get started again. Frankly, you may not get as attractive a job as you once had, and you may have to take less money than you would like. But if you follow the advice and the steps recommended in this book, you will get into a job situation that has good possibilities for more responsibility and more money. Consider a few examples.

A retired executive, now age 68, needs to work to supplement his pension income that, for whatever reason, has become inadequate. At the peak of his career, he was an outstanding manager of people and producer of superior results for several organizations. Now, however, after six months of fruitless efforts to find a managerial job appropriate to his worth, he has become discouraged and perhaps somewhat bitter. What might he do?

He might start his own small business or consider investing in a franchised operation. Further, he might try advertising his services as a management consultant. On a more direct, more practical level, he could do well to take the best job he can get, at whatever it might pay, that offers clear opportunities for advancement.

Retirees who take low-paying jobs often move up to management quickly.   For example, retired men of good health who are willing to work the night shift are in demand by many convenience store chains. The starting clerk salaries are not much more than minimum wage, and the job involves not only waiting on customers, but shelving and marking merchandise, sweeping floors, and cleaning counters, storage areas, and restrooms. It is seemingly not a very appealing picture, but with a former executive's experience and mature viewpoint, he will understand and appreciate—far more than the youngsters working in the store—the importance of being to work on time, not missing days from work, working hard, and cheerfully doing whatever has to be done.

The turnover among young people in these operations is very high, and it will not be long before the former executive rises to the top of the staff and is awarded a managership. Such organizations measure their success by their growth rate, creating additional district manager and regional manager positions time and again. With continued good health, the probability is very high that this man will in a few years be working in the organization's executive hierarchy and not sitting at home ranting at how his age is unfairly keeping him from getting a managerial job. Adjustment is often needed to obtain a goal.

Office skills training　　Now consider the case of a woman, a former department store buyer and section manager, recently widowed, and unable to live on her small Social Security pension. Now in her late fifties, department store personnel smile politely at her and say, "You have a very good background. We'll certainly keep your application on file and give you a call when we have a suitable opening." What happens next? Nothing, of course.

Perhaps she lacks the money or desire to start a small business of her own, and she has no office skills or experience. What might she do that has a good chance of paying off for her? Certainly she should consider getting some office skills training. Courses in beginning and advanced typing plus a basic course in computers will open some doors to good jobs, even for the mature applicant. After having learned keyboard skills and something about computer operations, other possibilities emerge. The foundation has been laid to take a course in travel agent work, for instance. All these types of jobs involve sitting at work rather than standing a great deal of the time, as in department stores or even gift or flower shop work.

Finally, how about the older person who has had many years of experience working as a mechanic or a construction worker? Consider the problem facing this man: He is 72 years old and in good health except for some arthritis in his hands that bothers him if he tries to work very long at his trade. For financial reasons, he becomes urgently in need of some type of job—a job that involves limited demands for using hand tools.

As is so often the case, weaknesses in formal education may be at the root of this man's problem. One possible solution is to go back to school. It is not at all unusual to see senior citizens in class, strengthening their basic education skills or just taking courses to enrich their lives and help pass the time. In this man's case, his few opportunities are probably going to be limited to such low-paying jobs as working at a filling station, working as a night watchman, or doing light yardwork for people.

But by raising his basic education skills, another obstacle falls. With friends and contacts in the construction or mechanics businesses, good jobs as timekeeper, parts department specialist, tool salesperson, or inspector, for example, become realistic possibilities.

Flexibility, Imagination, and Determination

If these or other common obstacles are in the way of your getting a good job, you may be able to break through such roadblocks by sheer persistence and more and more applications and interviews. However, more often you will have to reach your goal by applying your imagination and finding ways to go over, under, or around your obstacles. Essentially, you improve your qualifications by more education and training to qualify you for positions for which applicants are in high demand. You improve your personal appearance in every way. You learn to cope successfully with bad employment references as described in Chapter 5 and by use of the other methods described in this chapter.

Unemployable people.   There are almost no unemployable people. Flexibility, imagination, and ingenuity all are important in achieving your goal in spite of any handicaps that make your success far more difficult to attain than the average person's. If you can't get what you want with one method or going in one direction, change your methods or directions, or even change your goal, possibly to one more attainable than your first one. But the most important gain you can make in terms of your employability is to identify honestly any obstacles that have been blocking your path to a good job and set about eliminating them.

Getting Professional Help

2

Getting professional help to get a good job is time consuming and sometimes hard on the ego. Often you must reckon with a price tag. The vast majority of people who conscientiously follow the information and suggestions contained in this book will succeed in attaining their goal on their own.

However, if you are still failing and frustrated after some reasonable period of trying on your own to eliminate any obstacles and applying the methods provided here, you may need to seek some professional assistance. For such cases, here is some information and some advice on how to get it.

Employment Agencies
Public agencies

Applicants can get advice and help from public and private employment services. State-operated employment service offices provide their services at no charge to you or employers. The vast majority of their vacancy listings fall into one of two categories: (1) low-paying, menial jobs, with few opportunities for advancement and (2) jobs that pay in the medium range, but for which qualified people are relatively scarce, such as secretaries, word processors, and computer experts. If you are qualified for the latter positions, you won't need much help.

However, call your local employment service office and make an appointment. Use the interview to seek advice and assistance. There is nothing wrong with taking whatever job referrals you can get. Of greater importance, however, is discussing frankly any problems and frustrations you have been having and asking for some specific advice and assistance. If you don't get some real help from the interviewer, ask to see the director or supervisor of the office. Most employment service offices have evaluation procedures or have arrangements with organizations that do provide such services—including community colleges, federal job training centers for veterans, and some universities—at little or no cost.

Some evaluation procedures of value include aptitude testing, resume critiquing, checking on references with present or past supervisors to locate any sources of problems, and helping to improve appearance and interview effectiveness. Unfortunately, not all state employment offices are as competent and responsive in these matters as they ought to be, but it is worth asking about.

Private agencies   There are several major kinds of private employment agencies. Some specialize in providing contract or temporary people. Others concentrate on construction labor and skilled trade workers or domestic help. Other private agencies are known as search firms. They make their money by searching for hard-to-find specialized talents, such as those required in the scientific or management fields. Most will not accept your application. Placement agencies that charge a fee are most likely to be of help to you.

More and more states are outlawing registration fees. Many states now have passed laws that forbid such agencies from charging a registration fee. At one time many job seekers were charged registration fees and got no results.

Pay, if money is not a big problem.   As with other types of services, some do an excellent job and can really be a big help to you. Their fees are generally about ten percent of the annual salary of the position in which you are placed. Some will demand the fee in full, up front, possibly helping you arrange to borrow the money. Others will let you stretch the payments out over several months. Once in a while, the employer will pay the fee, but may then deduct part or all of it out of earnings over a period of time.

Be forewarned: Read the fine print and ask questions about anything that is not clear to you. Otherwise, you may find that you will owe the full fee if the job is eliminated, if the employer terminates you for cause, or if you soon learn the job was not what it was represented to be and you leave it. If you don't pay up, the agency can take you to court, get a judgment, and attach your wages when you do get a job. The agency also can enter a black mark on your record with local credit rating agencies.

Be wary of agencies that try to charge you for services such as preparing a fancy resume. This should not be necessary if you follow the suggestions and models set forth in Chapter 5. Some charge hefty fees for making and mailing hundreds of copies of applicants' resumes. Only in the very rarest of instances does that pay off even with some interview opportunities. Most organizations receiving unsolicited resumes through the mail simply discard them. If they don't, the chances that yours will hit the right person in the right organization at the right time are less than slim. If you are going to shop for a job by mail, you can save money by doing it yourself and increase your likelihood of success by reading the suggestions in Chapter 5.

Guidance Counseling and Testing
Be open and honest

It is absolutely essential that you open up to the individual who is trying to assist you. Talk honestly about what you see as the obstacles that have been keeping you from getting one of the better jobs that you have been seeking.

Test data will help, but nothing will be of more importance in the end than attaining a close understanding and rapport between you and your guidance counselor.

Guidance counselors can offer extremely valuable information and a lot of practical advice to people who are stuck in dead-end situations and who are undecided about career decisions. They have vast resources available, such as booklets and pamphlets that describe the nature, advantages, and disadvantages of almost every conceivable field of work. They are employed in high schools, colleges, universities, and some vocational or technical training centers, where their services are usually free. Some are in private practice. They charge for most of the help they offer, but their services may be well worth the price if you can afford them.

You will have no trouble finding a guidance counselor. Tell the receptionist at the institution of your choice what you need and make an appointment. For private counselors, check in the yellow pages.

Aptitude tests

If you are undecided about what field you think you want to get into, specifically ask your counselor to arrange some aptitude tests. A number of different tests, referred to as a battery of tests, may be needed.

Aptitude tests give you a good picture of your natural abilities. A number of such tests indicate hand and eye dexterity, mechanical ability, memory, reasoning or logic, social abilities, and other psychological traits.

Educational achievement tests

Educational achievement tests are also important because they measure both the type and amount of information that you have retained from your formal education. They are very useful in highlighting any deficiencies in math, writing, reading, spelling, and grammar that may be holding you back.

These tests can prove invaluable to the counselor and to you for considering alternative career fields and for determining the amount of remedial education that you may need before you can handle more advanced education or training.

Educational Counseling

Guidance counselors can guide in the selection of a career field. After you have decided on the type of job that you want to prepare for, you will benefit from educational counseling, which can help you in selecting courses and majors and identifying and evaluating the institutions and organizations that you may wish to consider.

State or private school?

Almost all state colleges and universities charge somewhat less than similar private institutions because they are subsidized by the state. However, cost may not be your only consideration. For example, convenience of location from your home may be a deciding factor because commuting long distances or living on campus can be quite expensive.

Accreditation

How do you know if a college or university is right for you? To a large extent, you will have to rely on your counselor for advice and information. State institutions are virtually always accredited, meaning that they meet certain academic and administrative standards set by the state's department of education. This is also true of most, but not all, private colleges. Information about accreditation can be obtained from the department of education. Generally, accredited institutions provide a higher standard of education. Perhaps most important, credits that you earn at an accredited institution are more likely to be recognized by other schools that have earned their accreditation.

Nonaccredited institutions may be able to do an excellent job for you, but be sure that they are state licensed. Your local Chamber of Commerce and Better Business Bureau can help answer that question and will know if any formal complaints have been lodged against the organization.

Commercial schools or training companies

Many commercial colleges and training companies do an outstanding job of preparing individuals for good-paying jobs and then assisting with placement. These may include secretarial schools, academies of hairstyling, pilot training centers (some of which can take students up to the commercial pilot level), and companies that offer hands-on training as well as theory for commercial truck operations, construction equipment operations, and maintenance.

Investigate and evaluate any commercial training organization before you sign up or pay any money. While most are legitimate, provide thorough, competent, and practical instruction, and are able to find good jobs for most of their graduates, some are run by fast-buck operators. Pay a visit to your local Chamber of Commerce (don't just phone) and ask about the reputation of any commercial training organizations you are considering. Your Chamber of Commerce can put you in touch with the local Better Business Bureau, where you will be able to learn about complaints that may have been lodged against the organization.

In addition, ask the school for the names and phone numbers of a few of its graduates. Talk not only to them but ask those graduates for the names of a few others. This way, you will quickly learn how good the training was and how good the jobs were that its graduates got.

Professional Associations and Organizations

If your questions are not answered or your need for referrals to local professionals who can help you has not been met, here is a list of associations and other organizations you can write to or call. They will help in any way they can.

Career counseling and testing

American Psychological Association
750 1st Street, NE, Washington, DC 20002. Has more than 50,000 member psychologists. Supports research in all phases of counseling and testing. Can provide names of member psychologists local to most areas.

American Vocational Association
1410 King Street, Alexandria, VA 22314. Distributes information on vocational, technical, and practical arts education, including programs sponsored by states and the federal government.

Community Guidance Service
133 E. 73rd Street, New York, NY 10021. While this is a New York City service, it can help with suggestions on how to locate similar community center services in other urban areas.

Independent Educational Counseling Association
Box 125, Forestdale, MA 02644. This is an organization of private counselors who work directly with students and parents. They not only provide testing and evaluation services, but also recommend schools.

Vocational Industrial Clubs of America
P.O. Box 3000, Leesburg, VA 22075. With clubs in most states, the VICA tries to interest young persons in trades and in technical, industrial, and health service careers.

Handicapped, older persons, women

Association for Persons with Severe Handicaps
11201 Greenwood Avenue, N, Seattle, WA 98133. Promotes and has information on such services as education, training, and rehabilitation for individuals with severe handicaps.

American Rehabilitation Counseling Association
5999 Stevenson Avenue, Alexandria, VA 22304. Serves as
liaison between private and public rehabilitation counselors of the handicapped.

*HEATH (Higher Education and Adult Training for the
Handicapped)*
One DuPont Circle, NW, Washington, DC 20036. Acts as a
clearinghouse of information on education and training
and promotes scholarship programs for the handicapped.

Forty Plus Club of New York
15 Park Row, New York, NY 10038. Assists individuals
more than 40 years of age who have executive or professional experience and a record of high earnings. Aids in
the preparation of resumes and developing interview and
campaign skills. Offers job counseling and arranges interviews and other consulting services. While generally a
New York City service, some free materials are available
to others.

Council on Aging
409 3rd Street, SW, Washington, DC 20024. Sponsored by
the National Council on the Aging, its purposes are to improve employment opportunities for older workers, promote understanding of older workers' capabilities, and
serve as advisor to older workers and older-worker employment services.

Wider Opportunities for Women (WOW)
1325 G Street, NW, Washington, DC 20005. Fosters expanded employment opportunities for women through information programs, employment training, and advocacy
services. Sponsors the Women's Work Force Network, a
national network of 350 women's employment programs.

Federal programs *Bureau of Apprenticeship Training*
Room: N-4649, U.S. Department of Labor, 200 Constitution
Avenue, NW, Washington, DC 20210. The Bureau admin-
isters Apprenticeship Training, the Job Training Partner-
ship Act of 1982 (JTPA), the Job Corps, programs for the
handicapped and economically disadvantaged, and the
Senior Community Service Employment Programs for
older workers.

Human Resources Development Institute
815 Sixteenth Street, NW, Washington, DC 20006. Works
to ensure full labor participation in employment and training programs funded under the JTPA. Assists in develop-

ing JTPA programs for dislocated and economically disadvantaged workers. Is associated with the AFL-CIO.

National Alliance of Business
1201 New York Avenue, Washington, DC 20005. Works to solve problems of unemployment by involving businesses in education and training programs that serve individuals facing barriers to employment.

Canadian information

Public Service Alliance of Canada
233 Gilmore Street, Ottawa, ON, Canada K2P OP1.

Canadian Rehabilitation Council for the Disabled
45 Sheppard Avenue E, Suite 801, Toronto, ON, Canada M6G 1L2.

Engineering Institute of Canada
2050 Mansfield Street, Suite 700, Montreal, PQ, Canada H3A 1Z2.

Canadian International Development Agency
200 Promanade du Portage, Huff, Canada K1A OC4.

Additional U.S. information

National Center for Job Market Studies
P.O. Box 3651, Washington, DC 20007.

National Employee Counseling Association
5997 Stevenson Avenue, Alexandria, VA 22304.

National Job Corps Alumni Association
607 14th Street, NW, Washington, DC 20005.

National Association for the Physically Handicapped
6140 Lafayette Avenue, Cincinnati, OH 45220-1000.

Worksheet: Obtaining Career Guidance Information

Using the categories below, visit a guidance counselor and seek answers and additional related data.

Counselor's Name _____ Tel. No. _____ Date _____

Address _____

Plan on starting with at least two occupations or specific positions to which you aspire based on your own analysis of your interests and aptitudes or as the result of professional testing and advice, as may be available.

FIRST PREFERENCE: _____

1. What special preparation will I need? _____

_____

2. How much money will it take to get the needed preparation? _____

3. How long will it take to qualify for an entry-level position? _____

4. Where in this area can I get the required preparation? _____

_____

5. What are some specific ways and places where I may be able to get financial help? _____

_____

6. What is the current annual starting pay in this field? _____ How much do people with five years' experience earn? _____

SECOND PREFERENCE: _____

1. What special preparation will I need? _____

_____

2. How much money will it take to get the needed preparation? _____

3. How long will it take to qualify for an entry-level position? _____

4. Where in this area can I get the required preparation? _____

_____

5. What are some specific ways and places where I may be able to get financial help? _____

_____

6. What is the current annual starting pay in this field? _____ How much do people with five years' experience earn? _____

How to Get Leads and Appointments: The Private Sector

What is a lead? As used here, getting a lead refers to finding out where there is a specific job opportunity for which you qualify and for which you would like an interview. As the heading indicates, this chapter is concerned with getting valuable leads in the private sector, meaning with commercial businesses and industrial concerns.

The next chapter offers similar help in finding good leads for jobs in government agencies.

The Classified Ads

The daily newspaper classified ads are the most productive source, numerically, of job leads. Here are some suggestions to help you make the most of the time and effort you put into working the classified ads.

Placing Your Own Classifieds

If you have a little money you can afford to gamble, by all means place a "Situation Wanted" ad in your local paper or papers. Write only about your "paper qualifications," that is, your education and work experience. Do not mention that you are attractive and personable and get along very well with people. If you're a woman, you may get some nuisance calls. If any should harass you, threaten to report him to the police.

Start your ad with the title of the job you want, such as "Teacher, Licensed," "Dental Lab Assistant, Experienced," "Secretary, with Good Shorthand," "Computer Programmer, Various Systems," "Child Psychologist, M.A." Follow the title with just a few lines more about your education and experience. If you wish to mention salary level, consider adding something like: Most recent salary $21,500. The danger is that doing so may rule out some calls. The advantage is that you will not likely be bothered with calls from those who will not meet your needs.

A tracking system. With a tracking system, you will proceed much more efficiently, thus getting more results for the time you spend. Clip all the ads that interest you. Paste them into a notebook or on 3×5-inch cards. Enter the date each appeared and later note the results of calls or other responses. These notes ought to include the names of people you talk with, phone numbers, and what happened at each contact, such as "job already filled" or "pay too low for me." If you get appointments, jot down the dates, times, directions for getting there, results of interviews, names of receptionists, interviewers, or others you have met. Doing this will prevent you from wasting time calling on ads that appear again and again. Your system will also be of great value to you for follow-up when you get interviews that don't result in an immediate offer.

Respond early. The better jobs don't lie around for long. Lots of people are looking for the good jobs, and lines form quickly. One employer had more than 200 calls a day for several days in response to a classified ad for an interesting, attractive job. People doing the recruiting have to cut off the supply arbitrarily when they accumulate an adequate number of apparently well-qualified callers. The same employer has often been nearly overwhelmed with responses by mail after using an ad that listed a box number. By the end of a week, it is not unusual to receive more than 100 letters and resumes for a good job opening.

When hiring, companies are often in an emergency situation and need to get the position filled quickly. If a well-qualified person among the first dozen or so applicants emerges, the job is often filled. So if applicants don't get their oars in early, very early, their chances drop off dramatically. If an ad says call between 9 a.m. and 2 p.m., for instance, start calling no later than 8:45. After placing such an ad, it is not unusual for the phone to start ringing at 7:30.

Be the earliest. Few employers will resent your early call if you offer a good reason. If it is a good job, the chances are it will be filled the first day, so waste no time in calling. Suppose your job requires you to report early, but you are committed to getting a better one. When you call on ads before you leave home, it is so early you get no answers. Try stopping on your way to work and using a public phone. If it is still too early, leave work for a few minutes and use a nearby pay phone. If that is impossible you may have to take a few hours off to compete with people who are also pursuing the better jobs. If your newspaper is not delivered early enough, see if you can get one sooner at a local newstand. However you work it, start calling early.

Effective Phone Calls

When you reach someone by phone with whom you can discuss a job opening, you are in a mini-interview situation. It has been said many times you have only one chance to make a good first impression. Here is how you do it.

Be organized

Have the ad in hand with paper and pen nearby. Write rapidly so you don't have to ask the person to repeat what was said. Avoid asking how words are spelled. If you don't know how to spell "Persimmon Street," do what you can with the way the word sounds. You can find out the correct spelling later. Remember, you are trying to sound smart, reasonably well educated, and fully alert.

Have things arranged so there are no background noises or distractions. It makes a bad impression on the person at the other end if your children are screaming, or dogs are yapping. In advance of your call, do whatever is necessary to make sure you won't have those problems. Children probably won't always heed your orders, and you may be tempted to lock the whole gang in a closet. Make them understand it is important for them to be quiet while you are on the phone. If nothing else seems to work, see if a neighbor will take them for an hour or so while you do your calling, or send them out to play if that is practical.

Talk cheerfully and confidently   The person you will be talking with can't tell whether you are plain, beautiful, or handsome, but you will project a mental image of yourself by the sound of your voice. Speak pleasantly, with self-assurance. If you feel you have a somewhat squeaky voice, try speaking in a lower tone. It will add resonance, and you will sound more attractive. Ask a close friend or relative if your voice sounds harsh or nasal. If it does, it may be to your advantage to work with a voice therapist or elocutionist. It is critical that you get over, under, or around this first hurdle.

Try to get information about the job before you talk much about yourself. It is most likely you won't have much time to talk on the phone, particularly if the ad is drawing a lot of responses. While your main objective is going to be an appointment to see someone about the job, you will also want to learn enough about the position so you can decide whether you want an interview. Also, the more you can learn about the job, the better you will be able to present your qualifications. The key to learning as much as you can in a short conversation is to ask questions. You can increase your chances of succeeding if you use an opening something like this:

> My name is Catherine Robinson and I'd like some information about the position you advertised in the paper today for a data processor. Can you tell me something about the duties?

If you find you are interested, show some enthusiasm. Every employer wants to hire people who are enthusiastic about the job and about coming to work for the organization. You don't need to bubble over, but if it seems it is a job you really want, give an honest reaction. Say something like, "That sounds great! It's exactly what I've been looking for! May I come and see you about it?"

Ask for a definite appointment.   The person you are talking with on the phone will have some questions to ask you because she or he won't want to waste time if you are not qualified or suitable. The employer may want to make notes of your qualifications and then call you back about an interview or a resume. Here is where it pays to be gently persistent and to use some initiative and ingenuity. Try to get a definite appointment without being aggressively pushy. For example, in your own words, say something along these lines if you haven't been invited to appear in person: "May I come by and talk with you about this and bring a resume with me? I can leave now and be there in about 20 minutes." Or, "Can you set up an appointment for me? I'd really like to meet you personally and explain how I can handle that job just the way you want it done." (If saying much of anything on the phone means that you are going to be saying "y'know" every few sentences, write a statement you can use for this purpose without any "y'knows" in it and read it to the person, having practiced it a few times to get it smooth.) This point of strategy is so important, we will present a bit of pretend dialogue to help illustrate the technique of being gently persistent but not aggressively pushy. If you are too aggressive, you can easily annoy and turn off people who are hiring. The trick is not to be too shy nor too assertive.

> *Applicant:* My name is David Thompson, and I'm calling in response to the ad in the paper for an accountant. I'd appreciate some information about the job. Could you give me the name of your organization? (Ask only if it has not already been provided to you, of course.)
>
> *Receptionist:* We're the Martin Steel Company. If you'll leave your name and phone number, someone will return your call later.
>
> *Applicant:* I'm sorry, I won't be where there is a phone most of the day. I guess I'll have to call back. Who shall I ask for?
>
> *Receptionist:* Well, Mr. Edmonds is doing the hiring, but he won't be in until this afternoon.
>
> *Applicant:* I see. I think I know your company. Isn't it located at the I-95 and Route 41 intersection?
>
> *Receptionist:* No, we moved from there. We're at 11160 Hampton Boulevard now.
>
> *Applicant:* Will the person who gets the job be working for Mr. Edmonds?

> *Receptionist:* No. He's an employment inter-viewer.
>
> *Applicant:* Do you have any idea when he may return this afternoon?
>
> *Receptionist:* I'm afraid not. He doesn't have a secretary and makes all his own appoint-ments.
>
> *Applicant:* Would it be all right if I stop in about 2:15 and take my chances that he'll see me when he gets back?
>
> *Receptionist:* I guess so, but you might have to wait around quite a while.
>
> *Applicant:* I'll do it. Could I stop by and say hello to you when I get there?
>
> *Receptionist:* Sure, I guess so. I'm Mary Greeley, and I'm on the reception desk in the lobby, so I suppose you'll see me here anyway. I'll be glad to give you a place to wait and intro-duce you to Mr. Edmonds when he comes in.
>
> *Applicant:* Thanks, Ms. Greeley, and I hope you'll mention to him that you said it would be okay if I stopped by to see him.

Being gently persistent does not always give you an ad-vantage over other applicants, but it works often enough to be worth trying just about every time. If you are offered an appointment for late in the day or perhaps for the next day, try to get a better one. You may have to make up an excuse if you don't have a good reason. That is up to you, but if the organization is under pressure to get the job filled—and it often is—those who are scheduled to be the tenth, twentieth, or thirtieth applicant to be interviewed have less and less chance of getting the job.

You can record the important information you gather from responding to classified ads on the worksheets at the end of this chapter.

Hand-carry responses　When an ad does not list a phone number but only a box number or an address, don't mail your resume. Take it per-sonally to the newspaper or the address given. Do it as early in the day as you possibly can. If the advertiser is hurting for a replacement, as when someone has left a key job suddenly, the responses will be picked up and reviewed very soon after the ad appears. The earliest responses will get first attention. The ones that arrive later may never even get opened. If, for some reason, you can't hand-carry your resume, do the best you can. Get your envelope to the post office immediately and send it special delivery or by express mail, if it is available.

Friends and Relatives as Leads

Classified ads are probably the most productive source of leads numerically. But in terms of the quality or value of leads, no other source approaches the worth of friends and relatives who have good jobs or who know someone. It should not be surprising that most jobs are not filled through classified advertising. One study made several years ago showed that 38 to 43 percent of jobs are filled by employee referrals. Only 21 to 25 percent are filled through newspaper advertising. The remainder are filled from miscellaneous sources, such as employment agencies and people who dropped by casually and left a resume before any vacancy occurred.

Employee referrals are such a major source of good applicants that some organizations pay their employees a cash bonus for recommending applicants who get hired. They do this for good reasons.

People who work in an organization usually know about the qualifications that are important to effective performance of many jobs there. Employees rarely recommend anyone unless they have confidence that the person they recommend has the ability or potential to perform the job well. They know that if they recommend a poorly qualified person, he or she will probably be screened out and not get the job anyway, and they will lose their reputation for having good judgment. Employers also like employee referrals because they save advertising costs and some of the time and effort of screening and interviewing candidates.

Let friends and relatives help. So when you decide to look for a better job, tell all your friends and relatives and ask them to keep their eyes and ears open for you. Don't let false pride get in the way of your doing this. It is no disgrace to want or need a good job. Millions of people finish school every year and enter the job market. Many more quit or are let go for one good reason or another. Use the people you know and who like and respect you to help you find leads. Few if any of them can get you a job or hire you. Getting the job is your assignment, but first you need leads; ask your friends and relatives to help.

Make new friends.   Suppose you don't have many friends or relatives, or the few you do have are not in positions to help you find leads. You can't create relatives, but you can make friends, lots of good ones if you are willing to make the effort and keep working at it. If you feel you are not very good at making friends, here are a few suggestions that will help get you as many friends as you have time for.

Introduce yourself to people freely, whenever appropriate. Use your name, get theirs, and jot down names so you won't forget them. Make an acquaintance out of your casual relationships with cashiers, store managers, bank tellers, and everyone you do business with. Smile and always have a few friendly words to say. Probe to see if there is some mutual interest between you that could lead to a friendship. You never know who will be able, directly or indirectly, to help your career along. Even if the acquaintances you make never are able to help, you will enjoy life more as you build and enjoy your circle of friends.

How about those who live around you in your private life? Take time to make friends with people who live in your apartment building or those who live in your neighborhood, if you live in a house. This is important in terms of your present job-finding campaign and also for the benefit of your long-term career goals. Perhaps you never even nod or speak when you see each other unless you almost collide in passing. Perhaps you don't like some things about many of them. If you get to know them better, you will probably find more likeable things about them than you had expected. It is well worth a try to strike up an acquaintanceship at least.

The next time you see one of them, even at a distance, wave and greet them. A little later on call out to them, go over and shake hands, and introduce yourself. When new people move in down the hall, next door, or even across the street, stop by and welcome them. If you feel too shy for that, get their names and send them a brief welcome note. You will be more than just surprised. You will be amazed at how warmly people respond to a simple, thoughtful act such as that. You will find yourself on the way to a new, enjoyable, and perhaps valuable friendship in many instances.

Throw a party.   If you can afford it, give a party now and then. Should you bring up the subject of your job search at such occasions? Certainly, if you want to, but don't try to pressure anyone. Some of your guests will probably ask how you are doing anyway. Be truthful. Ask them to let you know if they hear of anything opening up anywhere. Then, unless the person picks up the ball, change the line of conversation. If he or she does think of something later on, you will probably get a phone call.

Make new friends on your job.   Make more friends where you work. Later in this book we will talk about how to improve your chances of getting a better job right where you are working. But as a preliminary step, build up your list of friends in the same organization. If you are working in a medium-to-large organization where there are other departments, branches, or sections, the more friends you have throughout the place, the better will be your chances of learning about job opportunities. In some cases, a good friend may put in a word for you and tilt the decision in your favor. Reach out and get to know people not only in some sections but in all that you can, including the personnel or employment office.

If you find yourself on an elevator alone with another employee who is a stranger to you, introduce yourself. If you go to the cafeteria by yourself and there are no vacant tables, don't look for a table with employees you already know. Go to one with an empty place where strangers are seated. Introduce yourself, and ask if you may join them. When you learn someone in another department is getting married, drop by, introduce yourself, and wish him or her happiness. Congratulate someone in another office or department who has just returned to work after having had a baby.

If the organization has any social get-togethers, use them as opportunities to meet people and make more new friends. If you feel hesitant about introducing yourself to someone who has a prominent job in the organization, see if you can find someone to introduce you.

We have placed a lot of emphasis on building up your circle of friends in both your private and business life. It is probably the single best way to get leads about job openings for which you will have the inside track. Many organizations have a high percentage of employees who are related to each other or who got in through a friend working on the inside. If you want a better job, let the friends you have help you while you are building more and more friendships for the future.

Calling on Employment Offices

This section will help you become successful in making "cold calls" to various types of employment offices. You are making a cold call when you walk in without an appointment and ask to see someone about getting a job. This differs from the situation in which you have been screened by phone for a job that has been advertised or about which you have otherwise learned.

It is not easy to get a good job right away by walking in. It is a rare occurrence for someone to get a good job this way, at least immediately. Nevertheless, because it works once in a while and more often leads eventually to a better position, you might want to try it. You may not get anything more than an employment application to fill out. You may be told that there are no job openings in your line of work. However, if you have the time, make some cold calls.

State employment offices

The U.S. Department of Labor subsidizes the establishment and operation of free state employment offices to help people get leads to jobs in the private sector. Not very long ago these offices got almost no job listings for other than low-paying labor or clerical jobs.

In recent years, however, they have upgraded their job listings to better serve people qualified for technical, semi-professional, administrative, and some professional jobs. Even so, relatively few employers list their higher-paying jobs with state employment offices. Generally if they do, it is because they are desperate for skills that are scarce. Electronics engineers and technicians, computer programmers, and computer repair specialists are examples of the kinds of people who are almost never on file with these agencies.

If you have no special education or training and no significant experience or can be comfortable working for the time being at close to minimum wage, by all means register at your local state employment service.

Many people have gotten started by taking one of the jobs the service lists and then have worked up to better jobs. Furthermore, if you have typing or secretarial skills or some experience in mechanical work, you will have a good chance for a referral. One important advantage these agencies offer is their services are free.

Private employment agencies

Private employment agencies have much better listings of higher-paying jobs than state employment service offices. And some of the jobs they offer are fee paid—there is no charge to you unless the agency has registration fees. The employer pays for the agency's services when it hires someone who was referred by the agency. When this is not the case, the fees you will be charged may be higher than you can or want to pay. Ask questions about the fees of any agency with which you may deal and do it before signing anything; get a copy of the fee schedule to bring home.

Private employment agency fees vary considerably. At the low end, they charge about five percent of your first three to six months of earnings on any job for which they give you a lead and which you get. On a salary of $5,000 over six months, you would pay about $250. On the higher end of the scale, some charge as much as ten percent of your first year's earnings. For a job paying $20,000 a year, the fee would amount to about $2,000. Some agencies like to be paid as soon as you have been hired, but most will settle for payment over several months. Some will have you sign a statement waiving your legal rights. This can mean they have the right to garnishee your paychecks without much in the way of formalities. In many cases you will be liable for the fee even if you get fired or quit after a short while.

Read the fine print! Be sure you understand the conditions attached to fee-paid leads. Let's say the fee is to be paid by the employer, but payment is based on the employee being satisfactory and remaining on the job for a specified minimum number of months. Under such arrangements, if you don't like the job and quit after you have started, or if for some reason the employer lets you go after a short period, you may be liable for paying the fee.

If the lead is a good one and you get the job offer, the fee-paid arrangement may involve your paying, with the employer then reimbursing you in monthly installments or in a lump sum after an indicated number of months.

Employment agencies are most successful in providing leads to applicants who have skills, training, or experience in high demand. Secretaries in general and legal and medical secretaries in particular are relatively easy to get listings for. This is also true of skilled technicians, such as those in the dental/denture field, and for electronics, crafts, and computer jobs. In high-demand categories, qualified applicants can usually find employment on their own without much trouble. But private agencies many times can get them leads to better jobs than they can find for themselves.

However, a great many people who register with these agencies have employment handicaps, covering much more than physical disabilities. It is a handicap to have poor reading and computational skills or not to be able to speak reasonably good English, as with many foreign-born persons. Other handicaps that are barriers to getting good jobs, regardless of whether the barriers are legal, include being elderly, overweight, or tall, having bad teeth, and being a female or male for certain types of jobs.

Employment agencies often not only fail to help people with such handicaps, but also are unable to find productive leads for those with no special qualifications or who have a bad employment history. A bad history can mean having been fired from one or more jobs or having been a job-hopper whose employment record shows he or she seldom stays in a job for very long. Most employment agencies are negligent about checking out applicants' employment histories to verify past jobs and salaries and to get performance evaluations from previous employers. They will sign up almost any applicant and provide whatever leads are available. But when the employing organization checks the applicant's background, the person just does not get the job.

The point is, if you have an employment handicap or bad employment history, there is not much hope in employment agencies. If you know you have such a problem, start a vigorous self-improvement program and stick with it. If a bad employment history is dragging you down, take whatever job you can get at whatever salary you can survive on. Then, as quickly as possible, build a reputation as a valued employee. That, after a period of time, can serve as a springboard to better jobs.

Company employment offices

Medium and larger companies have their own employment staffs, which are usually part of a personnel organization. If you make cold calls to these places, you will almost always be treated with courtesy and consideration. This is because many companies make, distribute, or sell customer products. They see each applicant as also being a customer, or a prospective one, and are conscious of the importance of good public relations. If you believe such companies in your area have jobs you are qualified for, make them a major target. You don't have to wait for them to advertise. Stop by. In most cases you will get at least a courtesy interview and be given an application to complete and leave for their files. Naturally, the chances are slim when you walk in cold there will be just the kind of job you want and that you will be just the person they want for it.

When you get to talk with someone, ask how often people with your kind of qualifications are hired. The answer may be never or hardly ever, and you will want to spend your time and energies elsewhere. It is as important not to waste your time as not to take up other people's time needlessly.

Complete All Applications

Don't expect much from filing applications with employment offices. It is a good thing to do if a suitable vacancy occurs within a short time after you apply. Employment offices learn that applications on file get stale very quickly. For many reasons, recruiters will check only recent applications and then advertise. Nevertheless, there is nothing to be lost in filing a lot of applications where there are no current vacancies. But then don't sit back and wait for your phone to ring.

If you really want a better job, you need to keep working all the angles. Work the classified ads each day. Keep after your relatives and friends for leads, and make more new friends. Check out employment offices occasionally by phone or in person after you have provided them with a completed application. Learn the names of the interviewers or others you have met and call them by their names. Use courtesy titles—Mr., Mrs., or Ms.—unless you are invited to do otherwise. In checking back to see if a vacancy has occurred, don't make a pest of yourself. Most interviewers and others involved in the hiring process resent the time taken by overly persistent applicants. You will never get a job in an organization where the person who answers your calls rolls his or her eyes upward, turns to a nearby worker, and says aside, "It's that damn pest again!"

Read the Business Section

Watch the local newspapers for articles about companies expanding into new product lines or that have just landed a large contract. These reports are carried in the business and financial sections and sometimes make the front pages. They are usually a signal that additional people are to be hired in the near future. In addition to design and production jobs, expansion always means there will have to be more administrative support people. Do whatever you have to do to get your application in early. Don't just mail it in with a nice letter. Call by phone and try to get an appointment for an interview. If that doesn't work, consider making a cold call visit. If you barge in without an appointment, you may have to wait until someone is available to talk with you. If that is the only way you can get an interview, do it. Many employment offices handle applicants as if they were herds of cattle. Often such insensitivity is a tip-off to the attitude of the company's management toward people, including their own employees.

Be aware, however, that some applicants are now and then able to minimize this situation. They finagle appointments at the same time others are unable to get them.

It may seem unfair, but fairness is not everyone's watchword in competitive situations. What these people do is have a "story," one that may or may not be true:

> I have to work the same hours as your office is open, and we're so busy the boss won't give us more than an hour off at a time. I'll come any day you say, but I've got to have an appointment.
>
> I need to be sure I can see someone the first thing in the morning. The problem is I work way out of town, and I can't possibly get there before you close. If I can't be given an appointment, will someone stay late to see me?

This might be called a ruse or a ploy when it is not based on facts, and sometimes it does not work anyway. Let common sense be your guide.

Worksheet: Responding to Classified Ads by Phone

Using the record format below or using 3 × 5 cards, spend a morning calling in response to classified ads for positions that interest you and for which you qualify.

Type of position calling about: _____ Date _____

1. Phone number _____ Organization _____

   Address _____

   Special qualifications mentioned in the ad _____

   _____

   Person(s) talked with _____

   Results/impressions _____

   _____

2. Phone number _____ Organization _____

   Address _____

   Special qualifications mentioned in the ad _____

   _____

   Person(s) talked with _____

   Results/impressions _____

   _____

3. Phone number _____ Organization _____

   Address _____

   Special qualifications mentioned in the ad _____

   _____

   Person(s) talked with _____

   Results/impressions _____

   _____

4. Phone number _____ Organization _____

   Address _____

   Special qualifications mentioned in the ad _____

   _____

   Person(s) talked with _____

   Results/impressions _____

   _____

Worksheet: Personal Contacts

It is very important that as you establish leads, you keep a record of people you have talked with and how they might be able to help you in your job search. Use the following format to keep track of your personal contacts.

Sample: Name <u>Sue Germano</u>

Address <u>239 Oak Street, Rochester, New York</u>

Telephone <u>(210) 555-8731</u>

Source of contact <u>Joe Germano's sister</u>

Method of contact <u>I called her at work.</u>

Date(s) of contact <u>11/16</u>

Results/follow-up <u>She asked me to send her a resume. Sent 11/18. Call her 12/2.</u>

Contact 1: Name _____

Address _____

Telephone _____

Source of contact _____

Method of contact _____

Date(s) of contact _____

Results/follow-up _____

Contact 2: Name _____

Address _____

Telephone _____

Source of contact _____

Method of contact _____

Date(s) of contact _____

Results/follow-up _____

Contact 3: Name _____

Address _____

Telephone _____

Source of contact _____

Method of contact _____

Date(s) of contact _____

Results/follow-up _____

Going After a Government Job

Government jobs are good jobs. This chapter will give you important information and special pointers on how to get a job with the federal, state, county, city, or town government—civil service or political.

In terms of pay, benefits, working conditions, and job security, government jobs are among the best in the nation. People sometimes get laid off due to budget cuts, and a few are fired, but this is also true of employment in the private sector. In general, federal-level jobs pay better than those at the state level, and salaries tend to be lower as you move to county and local levels. However, in spite of common impressions to the contrary, most government jobs pay as much as or more than comparable jobs in business and industry, except possibly at the very highest management levels.

Some government jobs at all levels are filled and emptied according to the desires or whims of politicians who are in control at the time. Most government jobs, however, are filled through merit system procedures.

Also of great importance is the fact that in addition to many good-paying clerical positions, government agencies employ thousands of people in jobs that require advanced degrees. A few examples are weather experts, engineers, a wide range of specialists in the medical field, space scientists, and educators.

Other factors that apply to almost any government employment include super benefits compared to jobs with small businesses, and even most larger firms.

A second very important advantage lies in the unusually strong bonds of security that government jobs have. While almost all departments and agencies have to live with occasional budget cuts, they are nearly always permitted to reduce their employment levels through attrition. That means gradually reducing numbers of employees by routine departures. For example, in time a number of employees will go into retirement; some will die; others will resign to take jobs elsewhere. No one or almost no one has to be cut off by the pink-slip method.

Further, after you pass the probationary period of usually six months to one year and are rated as a satisfactory performer, a presumption is established that you will continue to perform satisfactorily. If you need additional training or supervision, it is provided at government expense.

Even if charges are brought against you, such as by your supervisor, you will have the right of appeal. This may be to a board of review or even to the director of the agency. So, government jobs are some of the world's most stable and secure.

Understanding Merit Systems

Merit systems are designed to take politics and favoritism out of the hiring process. In applying for a merit system job, you should never be asked about your politics, religion, national origin, or personal views on any subject. Merit system principles are intended to eliminate or at least minimize all hiring considerations except those bearing on your qualifications to do the work and except for public policies or preferences.

In fact, considerations of public policy can and often do override qualifications for doing the work. The result is that many times the best-qualified applicants, in terms of education and experience, are not hired, while less-qualified applicants are hired. Understanding this can mean you will have a more realistic idea of your chances of getting a merit system job. If you qualify for a public policy advantage, you should be sure to make your eligibility for it quite clear. These public policy advantages include, in almost all civil service systems, the following preferences.

Preferences   *Veterans.*   Under all merit systems, an applicant who is an honorably discharged U.S. veteran is favored. This is usually accomplished by adding points to his or her eligibility rating. Thus, a veteran may be moved up ahead of nonveterans who possess superior paper qualifications. Paper qualifications include education and experience and the results of competitive tests of aptitudes, job readiness, and skills.

Disabled veterans.   Disabled veterans who meet the minimum qualifications for a given job are usually moved automatically to the top of hiring lists, sometimes over vastly better-qualified candidates.

Minority.   Where the goals of an affirmative action nature have been established, minority applicants are given preferential treatment over nonminority applicants who would otherwise get the jobs.

Women's preference.   For certain types of jobs where women are not traditionally found, females may be given preferential treatment.

State/city residence preference.   In some merit systems you must live within a certain area in order to be allowed to compete for government jobs. For example, a city or town may limit police or firefighter jobs to residents. This usually makes those living in the suburbs or other nearby towns and cities ineligible, regardless of qualifications. If it is important enough to you, perhaps you can move to its area.

Promotion-from-within preference.   Many years ago most government jobs at all levels were filled by open competition. This meant that when such jobs were created or became vacant any citizen had a chance to compete for them. People who were not already working for the government could apply and get consideration right along with government employees who also wanted to apply. The idea was to serve the best interests of the taxpayers by filling all openings with the best-qualified, most competent people.

This is no longer the case. Employees, employee groups, and government officials gradually squeezed out the competition from most of the middle-range jobs and the top jobs, except for certain scientific specialties.

Today, about the only chance outsiders have of getting a good government job above the lower-paying levels is when there are few if any people on the inside who want the job or are qualified for it. Typically, whenever a middle- or higher-level vacancy occurs in a government agency, special promotion boards are used to help screen and rate present employees interested in getting promoted to the position.

The net effect of this arrangement is as far as most outsiders are concerned, if they want to work for a government agency, they will have to start at or near the bottom. Occasionally a new department will be created or an existing one will expand rapidly. Then a number of people at the base and middle levels may have to be hired, usually on a temporary basis. Newspaper articles will usually tip you off to such rare events. Waste no time in applying.

Entry-Level Jobs

For recruitment and classification purposes, government jobs are generally grouped into three main categories. There are the professional positions encompassing law, medicine, scientific investigation and research, and higher-level executive positions. Administrative positions comprise such fields as accounting, purchasing, bookkeeping, computer programming and operation, and clerical. The third category is usually called crafts and custodial. This group takes in positions requiring carpentry, electrical and mechanical work, security, building maintenance, ground maintenance, and cleaning. Additional categories are used to provide for positions unique to the functions of certain agencies. Public health and welfare is an example, as is education for school systems, and transportation for departments that manage transit systems. The important point is to understand that there are special qualification requirements and often tests required of applicants according to the categories of jobs in which they are interested. From the examinations and ratings of education and experience, qualified applicants' names are put onto lists of eligibles.

Lists of eligibles   To get a civil service or merit system job, you will need to watch for announcements of examinations for the various categories of jobs. These are usually posted on a bulletin board in the organization's reception area. In most jurisdictions you can register at the recruitment or personnel office to receive copies of announcements about positions for which you would like to compete. However, it is better not to rely on being notified by mail. Personally check the posted listing frequently.

Passing a test.   To get on a list of eligibles you must complete an application and get a passing score on an examination for the type of position you desire. If you do well on the examination, your name will be on a list of those eligible for an appointment. You will be ranked on the list in accordance with how well you scored or were rated. Naturally, the higher you stand on the list the better; in general those at the top get the first available jobs. Your place on a list will reflect the numerical score you merited plus any public policy hiring preferences to which you are entitled.

Getting on a list does not ensure you'll get an offer.   Assume you responded to an announcement that an examination has been opened for a position for which you are qualified. You filed all the necessary papers, have already been examined, and have received a notice that you have been approved as eligible with a rating of 87.5. Sounds good, so far. Possibly, it is good, and perhaps you will soon get a letter asking you to appear and discuss an offer. But you may never get an offer from the examination. In fact, most of the applicants who have succeeded in getting their names on lists of eligibles never get a job offer from any of the lists. In rare instances, no one on the list will get an offer. This may result from a sudden change in program plans or funding within the agency. Normally, however, some people who are high up on the list will get hired, and some of those with middle-level rankings may get offers if large-scale hiring is going on or if high-demand skills are involved. Here are some of the reasons why you may not get an appointment, even though you came through with what seemed like a good score or rating.

Why you may not get an offer

Flexibility of selection. Normally, the part of the organization using a register for filling its jobs has some flexibility in selecting people from the active list. In some systems they are allowed to choose any of the five candidates who are nearest the top of the list. In other places they are limited to choosing one of the top three. So even if you head the list, it is possible to be passed over. When one of the top-ranked candidates has been hired, the others move up one notch on the list.

Discarded registers. Lists of eligibles tend to get stale after a time, just as do files of applicants in the private sector. When some significant period of time has passed, many of the people on a register will have gotten better jobs and no longer be interested in their eligibility. Some will have moved away from the area. Others will have married, will be in the process of raising a family, and will have decided they are not interested in being employed. Efforts to hire from stale lists can be frustrating, and often the decision is soon made to get candidates for a fresh list.

Elimination of the best-qualified candidates. The farther down the agency goes in selecting applicants from a list of eligibles, the weaker the qualifications of the candidates. Therefore, at some point before the bottom of the barrel is reached, the decision is usually made to reannounce the examination and recruit more and, the agency hopes, better-qualified candidates.

It is important for you to note these things if you are determined to have a government career so you can function to your best advantage. Be persistent and realistic. If you are on a list of eligibles and have what seems a good rating but get no word after several months, occasionally inquire if the register is still active. If it has been discarded, you will want to find out about plans to set up a new list. Don't count much on being notified automatically. In most cases you won't be, and if you are not alert, you can easily miss the filing deadline for the new list. Some examinations are conducted on an open-continuous basis, such as for typists and secretaries. Even with this arrangement you may not get an offer if your score or rating is not significantly above the minimum. New and probably better candidates are being rated all the time, and you may just sit there near the bottom or eventually get washed out. Get additional training and practice your skills until you become more proficient. Then be examined again to get your name moved up higher on the list.

It will be to your advantage to understand the difference between assembled and unassembled examination procedures. The more you know about how civil service organizations grade, rank, and hire applicants, the better you can make the most of what you have.

Assembled Examinations

Assembled examinations involve written or performance tests, and candidates are assembled in groups to take the exams. Written tests are used to obtain a measure of a candidate's knowledge, memory, and reasoning ability. Performance tests may be used to assess physical condition, agility, and coordination; they are used in recruiting for police or firefighter positions. They may also be used for testing a skill—typing, welding, stenography. If there is time between the date you are notified to appear for an exam and the date it will be held, use it to prepare yourself to earn a high score. Most people who are nervous before taking a competitive test settle down after the first several minutes and do just fine. If you do poorly because of apprehension, there are two ways to help you do better. The first is to study and practice the subject matter. The other is to take the test over and over, at different times, until you overcome the nervousness.

Various written tests

Many written or paper-and-pencil tests are supposed to measure learning ability, intelligence, or accumulated knowledge. The validity of some of these tests has been under attack for a long time, but many jurisdictions still use them. Almost all such test items can be answered better by applicants who did well in school. The theory is that by asking questions involving items such as arithmetical computations and history, the more intelligent applicants can be separated from the less intelligent ones.

The theory is suspect, but no matter. Experts disagree about whether you can do better if you practice taking such tests. The right answer is probably that practicing is at least somewhat beneficial. However, if you are weak in your knowledge and skill with math, English, and other basics, taking some courses in those subjects will help more than anything else. Here are some useful suggestions that can boost your score modestly on most general mental abilities tests.

Ways to boost test scores

Begin by moving quickly but thoughtfully through the entire test.   In doing this, answer all the questions that give you little or no difficulty. Don't spend a lot of time on any questions that have you stumped or are giving you a hard time. If any of the questions send you into a mind-lock, jump over them. First do the kinds of questions you are good at. Then spend your remaining time on the hard questions. This will prevent you from getting a lower score because you never got to many of the questions you could have answered quickly. Guessing won't help your score. The scoring procedure provides for subtracting the number of wrong answers from the number of right ones. Thus if you answer all questions just by guessing on a 100-item true-false test, for example, by luck you will get 50 right. Subtract 50 wrong from 50 right, and what score results? Zero.

If computations are required, doublecheck each of your answers. In trying to hurry, people make a great many careless errors that damage their scores. Blank paper is usually supplied. If not, use some blank paper you have brought with you or do your figuring in the margins of the test paper, but do each calculation twice.

Watch your time. You will be informed as to how much time you will be allowed for completing the test. Glance at the time now and then so you are able to pace yourself to get through the test. If you finish ahead of time, don't turn the test in until it is called for. Use all your remaining time to go back and check your answers. If you find and correct only a few mistakes, it can have a very important effect on your standing in relation to your competitors.

Study true-false questions for clues if you don't know the answers. True-false questions often contain clues to help eliminate guesswork. The most common clue words are *always* and *never*. These words can be accurately applied to very few things. You can make some gains usually by marking all such questions false. There almost always are exceptions to any statement. For example, if an item says, "It never rains in the Sahara Desert," and you don't know whether it does, mark the statement false.

Tests of keyboard skills It is standard practice for merit system employment staffs to give skill tests before qualifying applicants for jobs involving keyboard skills. Typewriters, computers, word processors, and teletypewriters all have essentially the same keyboard configuration onto which additional special keys are provided. If you can use a typewriter efficiently, there is an excellent rate of transfer of those skills to other similar types of machines. If you are to take a keyboard skills test, be sure you are familiar with the type of equipment to be used. Try to locate a similar machine that you can practice on. Ask friends who do office work. See if a local dealer will let you practice on one of its demonstrators. Most people will be surprisingly helpful in these situations if you explain your problem and ask in a nice way.

If you fail the first time you take the test, don't just take it over and over. Rent or borrow a machine if you don't have one and practice. As you practice, keep testing yourself. You ought to be doing at least 50 words per minute (WPM), net of errors, before you go to take an employment test. Your gross score is the total number of words per minute that you have typed. You get your net score by subtracting your error penalties from your gross score.

Practice keyboard skills before the test.   For the purpose of testing yourself in preparation for a civil service exam, a five-minute testing period is about right. Use as your test material some copy containing numerals and symbols as well as letters. Time yourself exactly, to no less nor more than five minutes. Count the number of letters and characters in each line and add them up. This will provide you with the number of strokes you have typed. An average word is considered to consist of five strokes. So divide your total strokes by five to get the number of average-sized words. Divide that number by the five minutes of testing time to get your gross WPM. You need to penalize yourself for any mistakes. The penalty rate is 25 strokes, or five words, per error. Search for, mark, and add up your mistakes. Multiply your total errors by five to get the number of penalty words. Subtract this from the total number of words typed. After deducting your penalty, what you now have is the net number of words you typed. Divide this figure by the number of minutes—five—your test ran, then you will arrive at your net WPM score. This is what really counts.

Test yourself at the end of each practice session, and keep records so you can enjoy your progress. Count your errors conscientiously. It is silly to cheat on yourself. A strikeover is still an error, as is using two spaces where one would be correct. If you leave out a period or a comma, mark it as an error. Be hard on yourself. It is the best way to improve your skill so that careless errors will not ruin your score. Keyboard skills lead to jobs where you can climb a career ladder if you keep learning and developing.

Tests for shorthand skills

Shorthand is an important secretarial skill today, but proficiency in it is rare. If you will take some courses and develop more than a passable shorthand ability, you will easily get good-paying job offers, provided your typing is also reasonably good. You can pick up shorthand or typing skills by buying a self-instructional book or getting one from your local library. But this is not as good as getting expert instruction. Self-taught shorthand is not as difficult to master as proficient typing, but it does take at least several hundred hours of hard, concentrated practice. The traditional methods of taking shorthand may be the fastest among the manual systems, but for most jobs you don't need to attain top speeds. Most people dictate at a relatively slow pace because they have to hesitate and think as they go along.

More recent systems use abbreviations and standard letters and symbols to represent words and phrases. These are shortcuts, used in lieu of the "curlicues" that are the hallmark of the traditional systems. If you can't afford the time and money to go first class, by all means take up one of the new, simplified shorthand methods. With practice, they will get you by most merit system entrance examinations. In making secretarial assignments from lists of eligibles, poorly or minimally qualified persons are not sent to work in the best and most important spots. You will achieve a better starting assignment if you develop your proficiency as well as you can before you take the examination.

Dictating machines and transcribing skills

Whether you have shorthand skills, it will be a big plus if you can indicate in your application that you are qualified to do transcription of machine dictation. The use of dictating machines to replace shorthand dictation has been growing steadily. Although not a skill usually included in preemployment testing, secretarial jobs involving machine dictation are becoming more commonplace. If the merit system to which you are applying has secretarial openings in which machine dictation is acceptable, you will probably be started at least one level above the grade and pay rate for clerk-typists.

Modern dictating and transcription machines are expensive. Rent one to learn and practice on if you can afford to. If not, inquire among your friends who are office workers. Most medium and large companies have such machines. Different ones have different features, but they are all basically the same. After you master one, the transfer to others is easy. In any event, it ought not to be difficult to use one to learn on if you have friends in organizations where they are used. If need be, ask to use a machine evenings and on weekends. As an added bonus for your efforts, you may find yourself with a good job offer from the organization where you have been using the equipment. Your ambition may attract attention, leading to a job offer.

Tests for trade jobs

Generally speaking, there is less emphasis on assembled examinations for journeymen carpenters, electricians, typewriter repairers, and painters. Holders of certificates from technical schools, unions, and company training programs with a substantial history of work experience are sufficiently qualified to be hired on an unassembled examination basis. In some cases, simple literacy and math exams are used for journeyman positions. Much more thorough written knowledge and aptitude tests are utilized in the selection of apprentices. Most government agencies have excellent training programs involving classroom, shop, and on-the-job training. These programs exist most often in areas with a shortage of qualified journeymen or with federally sponsored job training programs.

To learn more about these possibilities, stop at a local vocational school or write to the Bureau of Apprenticeship Training, Room: N-4649, U.S. Department of Labor, 200 Constitution Avenue, NW, Washington, DC 20210.

Tests of physical condition and skill

If you want a job as a police officer, firefighter, or lifeguard, you will probably have to take a simple written test to demonstrate your educational level. You will also usually be required to demonstrate your physical condition and skill.

You can benefit from preparing for a physical abilities test. Attend a test as a spectator to learn what to practice and how best to train for the tests.

These jobs are being sought by more and more women. While their failure rate is higher than that of men, things are changing. First, many pure strength requirements have been found excessive and are being modified. Second, women are doing a better job of preconditioning themselves for the tests and are becoming more physical in general. Witness their enormous strides in sports such as swimming, track and field, and gymnastics.

Bear in mind that assembled examinations are used almost solely for the lower, entry-level jobs. Unassembled examination procedures are the only ones used for rating candidates for the higher-level positions. As you recall, assembled examinations involve testing candidates, usually in groups, for their knowledge, mental abilities, or skills.

Because government agencies now have a very tight promotion-from-within policy for the better-paying jobs, few people get hired above entry level except in scarce-skill and technical/professional jobs. But there are advantages to getting inside and becoming eligible to compete for the middle- and higher-level positions, at some initial sacrifice.

You may find it will pay you handsomely, in the long run, to take a clerk or clerk-typist exam, even though in your previous jobs you were earning more and had greater responsibility. If so, the chances are good that you won't stay in a base job very long. Also, based on your previous experience and higher earnings level, most civil service systems have policies that provide for you to start above the minimum for an entry-level job in your field.

Administrative Intern Programs

Many civil service systems have special types of entry-level examinations for individuals with college degrees. Often referred to as administrative intern programs, their objective is to bring into the system bright college graduates who can get special training to move up career ladders in fields such as budgeting, purchasing, office services, and personnel administration. In most cases it is not a firm requirement to have a degree to be eligible to compete for these spots. However, extra points are given for higher education. Thus, even though you might do well on written tests, you will not do well on the overall basis if other candidates have more formal education. These entry-level jobs start at one or more grades above the lowest-paying jobs.

Because it is illegal to discriminate on the basis of age, unless age can be clearly established as an essential requirement, people who have been out of college for years are eligible to compete for those administrative intern positions. If they land one of the jobs, any relevant experience they have accumulated can help them get ahead faster than college graduates who enter with little or no experience.

Get started somehow, if only on a lower rung. College graduates who fail to get a job through an administrative intern program or who don't want to wait until the next examination is scheduled often use the clerk and clerk-typist route to gain entrance. In many cases they will have friends in one of the organizations served by the exam who are in supervisory positions. The supervisor will request the individual be assigned to his or her group as a clerk-typist, for example. Then almost immediately the entering person will be assigned duties more commensurate with his or her abilities, even though rated and paid as a clerk-typist. Most systems require new employees to stay at the same grade level for a probationary span of 6 to 12 months. Thereafter it is generally customary to enable them to skip a certain number of grades up the promotion ladder, provided they meet the qualification standards. Ordinarily they must compete with other eligible employees through the promotion boards or career panels.

Unassembled Examinations

Unassembled examinations usually consist of rating applicants on a point scale based on their relevant education and experience and then adding whatever preferences may be due them.

Most such procedures provide for giving applicants up to a specified maximum number of points for their related education. More points are then added for each year of generally applicable experience with additional points for directly applicable experience, always up to a set maximum. By using limits on points for experience, younger people are better able to compete with those who have compiled a great many years of experience, often at the same job and the same level.

Those who determine ratings are often permitted to add points if they deem the quality of an applicant's experience to be above average. It is important that you know and be guided by this basic information, because how high your rating will be on unassembled examinations depends almost entirely on how good a job you do in completing your application and any resume material you attach.

The Examination Announcement

Announcements of examinations for civil service jobs describe the nature of the work involved and explain the qualifications in education and experience. Study the announcement very carefully for any merit system job for which you are going to apply. While this is important in applying for jobs awarded on written or performance tests, it is even more important where all the rating points will be based on material you submit with your application. Not paying close attention to the announcement can mean you will lessen your chances.

Detailing Your Qualifications

In describing your qualifications for a merit system job, remember some or all of the rating will be on an unassembled basis, so always go into great detail. Fill up as much space as you can with information about relevant subjects studied and with information about each job you have held with any significant bearing on the job you are trying to get. Going into great detail will often earn you more points, as long as what you write bears on the requirements in the announcement.

It works out this way for two reasons. The first is simply salesmanship. And while good sales technique doesn't mean lying or bluffing, it does mean putting the product's good points in the most favorable light. Second, it will probably take extra details to show how your qualifications mesh with what the employer is seeking.

To illustrate these important points, assume that two young men have just finished high school together. Both are applying for the same job—insurance sales trainee. Neither has had any significant job experience, other than managing a paper route for several years. In addition to whatever other little experience they had had, each described his paper route work as follows:

> *Applicant 1.* Delivered papers for three years. Called on new neighborhood residents to see if they wanted to take the paper and then collected money due from subscribers. Collections were turned over monthly according to what the paper charged, and I was able to keep the difference.

> *Applicant 2.* As circulation and delivery boy for the *Delville Morning News,* had responsibility for selling the service to new residents as well as

those taking the rival newspaper. I put special, personalized notes on the new-subscription form supplied by the company and put them under the front doors of all the homes I considered to be prospects. Then one or two days later, I would stop by to see the people, explain a little about the *Morning News*, and leave them a free copy.

I would get their names and then later look up their phone numbers. If they didn't subscribe in a week or so, I would call and see if they would take a one-week trial subscription that the company offered. During the three years that I served this route, I sold 241 new subscriptions, which won me second prize one year and first prize another.

In addition to making daily deliveries, I kept careful records of nondelivery days, such as when subscribers were on vacation, and adjusted their bills accordingly. My subscriber billings were the basis for preparing monthly sales and deliveries reports, in which I computed costs, income, and any payments due to the company.

Using a scale of one to ten, how much would you assign to each of these applicants? Most civil service examiners would rate Applicant 2 far higher as a prospective salesperson. If you didn't, you would have a hard time justifying your decision to the chief examiner, who had given you your training and who would probably take you into a small room for a long talk about why you weren't doing as well as the other examiners.

Take this point seriously—in preparing your experience statements for merit system positions, write plenty about each job you have had, without being ridiculous, of course. Full and detailed statements can't hurt, and they will almost always get you more rating points and thus a better chance for the job you want.

Special Strategies That Sometimes Work

Selective certification

When a government supervisor or executive has a vacancy or is expecting one, a requisition is sent to the merit system or personnel office. If no employees are interested in or eligible for the job, the supervisor gets a list of applicants from a roster of eligibles who meet the requirements in the requisition. If these requirements are somewhat unusual, such as fluency in a foreign language, some knowledge of medical terminology, or training in the use of highly specialized tools or equipment, selection from the top may be waived. Thus the agency's rule that the supervisor must choose from among the top three or top five candidates, as is typical, may not apply if none of those applicants has the needed special qualifications. The supervisor may then go down the list to the first candidate who has the essential abilities and select that person.

This practice is generally known as "selective certification" and has legitimate uses, although it is subject to shenanigans at times. If a supervisor wants to hire a particular individual, a study of the job and the person's background may result in identification of some exceptional experience that can be magnified in importance beyond any sensible value. Nevertheless, the justification may get rammed through. The result sometimes is that the system gets short-circuited and the supervisor gets the favored person hired.

It is important to know about this because it should reinforce your need to describe your experience thoughtfully and in detail. In doing so, you may mention some special training or experience you have that will make you a legitimate choice for being certified on a selective basis.

Emergency and temporary appointments

Government agencies now and then receive legislative mandates that make it necessary to expand their staffs quickly to meet emergency needs. In these cases, any pertinent existing rosters of eligibles may be used up in short order. It takes substantial time to prepare new lists in the traditional way, and temporary appointments are often authorized until regular, new examinations can be held and the ratings completed. Hiring under temporary authorization still involves ensuring that those given such appointments have their applications examined and rated to be sure that they meet the minimum qualifications needed to perform the work. What is waived is the need to compete by ranking on the basis of test scores, education, and experience points.

If you are in the market for a better job and would like to obtain a government position, watch your local newspapers carefully for articles that will tip you off to the fact that a government agency in which you are interested has received a major new assignment. Swing into action immediately. Visit the nearest office of the governmental entity involved and get an application on file. If you already filed one some months ago, update it. These are golden opportunities. Employees inside the organization will be tipping off friends and relatives to apply. Supervisors, who may have a stack of completed applications stashed away in their desks or files, will root through them to help find candidates.

What about this temporary tag? Won't it mean that you will be out on the street after the term of your temporary appointment ends? Yes, it could. You may have a job you would have to give up. But if you take the temporary government job, you will have two big advantages in getting closer to your goal of becoming a regular government employee.

In the first place, temporary appointments have a way of getting extended for another period and then another one. During this time some attrition among the regular staff occurs. Some retire. Others quit or get fired. And it seems the staffing of virtually every government agency only goes one way, gradually up and up. In due course, many of the temporaries get converted to regular appointments. When regular appointments open up, those holding temporary appointments are usually exempt from having to compete for their jobs. They must be examined only to get certified. Next, even if your temporary appointment expires, you will have a leg up on getting a similar job in the agency through competitive appointment procedures. You will get credit for experience that exactly fits the duties and requirements of the job you held within the agency.

Incidentally, you would, of course, make as many friends as possible with other employees, supervisors, and personnel people while working under a temporary appointment. Good relationships can redound to your benefit if later you want a competitive appointment.

Formal promotion procedures

Promotion policies and procedures in almost all government departments and agencies are far more formal and structured than in all but a few private companies.

This can often be a big break for you, or you may compete and lose out enough times to discourage you. Don't turn away from the program on that basis.

In the first place, don't try for those for which you know you're not well qualified.

Second, even if you have good qualifications for the open position, face up to the fact that someone else may have great qualifications, so become philosophic about losing.

Finally, learn to work the system to your advantage. Prepare better resumes if you possibly can. Write more than a minimum. Look on the interview process as an opportunity to improve your interview performance. Each one is a performance, whether one likes it or not.

In most government organizations, the system works in the following way. When a vacancy happens or is known to be coming up, the personnel specialists, in collaboration with a promotion board, study the job and make up an announcement, usually posted on bulletin boards.

The announcement tells about the duties and responsibilities, describes working hours and conditions, and lists the qualifications being sought

After the applications are received, they are graded, and the three or five best qualified are chosen. Each is then notified of a desired date and time to appear for an interview.

Usually, the interview is individualized; that is, one candidate at a time meets with the promotion board. In a few instances a board may hold a group interview with all the top candidates present, but that procedure is not often used.

Apply whenever you feel you will be a strong candidate. Do great resumes. Tailor each somewhat to the job being offered. If and when you lose, try, try again, but perhaps more selectively.

Political Appointments   In politics individuals newly elected to government positions and some who are appointed to them have the right to fill some jobs by direct appointment. These positions are not under the merit system. Those who are hired to fill such jobs help to ensure that the ideologies and goals of the elected politicians are maintained. They serve at the pleasure of the official who appoints them, so they have little or no job security. Those empowered to make these appointments can, if they choose, appoint people who have no discernible qualifications for the positions. However, if done often, this results in public criticism, so usually an effort is made not to make completely indefensible appointments.

Despite the lack of security, these can be jobs that are interesting, exciting, and developmental. They also often carry fine salaries and generous benefits. And if the official who sponsors you is successful in getting reelected, such jobs can last for many years.

Earning a political appointment

It is possible to get appointed to a good job by a politician on the basis of nepotism or cronyism. But the world of politics operates on the basis of favors. Unless a politician you approach for a job happens to be a close relative or personal friend, something owed or earned must be involved. That is, you may get an appointment as a result of a past favor you or someone who is sponsoring you has done for the politician. If not, then you or someone sponsoring you has to be able to deliver a future favor.

Doing volunteer work

Unless you have good political connections you can call on, the way to enhance your chances of getting appointed to a good job is to do a favor yourself. If you don't have money you can donate to campaign funds, what you need to give is time and energy. Assuming you lack important connections with powerful politicians currently in office, your best opportunity is with individuals running for office. Volunteer your time to help the person get nominated or elected, as the case may be, when you first approach the candidate. Don't make your offer through other volunteers or paid campaign staff members. Almost without exception they will be feathering a nest for themselves. If they do anything for you, it will be to help their own cause.

Use your ingenuity to talk personally with the candidate and make your offer. If he or she is a very prominent person, it may take some doing to get your chance to make a personal pitch. For example, attend a meeting where the candidate will be making a campaign speech. Decide beforehand what you are going to say and practice saying it in a lively way. Use a strong but pleasant voice.

You might say something like this:

> I am Barbara Jackson, and I've been wanting very much to meet you. Would you let me come by your office and tell you something about my qualifications to work as a volunteer to help you get elected (or nominated, as the case may be)? I know you don't have time right now, but here is a card with my name, address, and phone. Would it be all right if I call your secretary and see when I can come and talk with you?

Few candidates will refuse to meet a potential volunteer. Assuming you get an affirmative answer, use a positive attitude when you call the secretary. For example:

> My name is Barbara Jackson. I talked with Ms. Kaplan recently at the Indian Trails PTA meeting, and she wanted me to call you and set up an appointment to see her personally about helping with the campaign. When would be a good date and time? Something in the next several days if at all possible.

Offer your services early

When you meet the person, have a resume with you detailing your experience and, if possible, a letter from a prominent party member or politician. The letter should vouch for the fact that you are a bona fide member of the candidate's political party as well as offer a personal recommendation. Be specific about the days and hours you can work. If you already have a job, you will have to plan on giving up some evenings and weekends. Again, show some personality as well as knowledge of the candidate's background and position on important issues so that you can carry on a knowledgeable conversation. If you are talking with a major candidate and you seem to be acceptable, you will probably be asked to call the campaign manager. You will not see the candidate on a daily basis. However, you will need to use every opportunity to make your presence and your work evident to the candidate.

It will be to your advantage to get into such campaigns early. The earlier you get to be a volunteer, the more interesting and responsible your assignments will be and the more chances you will have for a personal association with the candidate. After you do some volunteer work and begin to make yourself valuable, don't be shy about letting your objective be known. You hope to get a good job if the campaign is successful. Say it openly and frankly, more than once. Find out what those jobs will be, and pick one you would like to have and for which you have some evident qualifications. Then let everyone know that is the one you have your eye on.

It is important to establish your territorial objective early. Otherwise someone else will speak for the job before you do. If you learn the job you picked is already spoken for and committed to someone else, pick another job and stake a claim to it.

Keep detailed records   File away receipts of any unreimbursed expenses and make notes on everything you accomplish. Then give the candidate a brief written report every now and then, summarizing your accomplishments and suggesting what else you would be glad to do to help.

Worksheet: Exploring Government Job Opportunities

Using the format provided below, select a specific government position and government agency—federal, state, county, city, or town—and obtain information on the possibilities and procedures for obtaining a position of the type you would like to have and for which you are qualified.

Type of position calling about: _____ Date _____

1. Phone number _____ Agency called _____

   Address _____

Ask and summarize answers:

1. How may I obtain information about obtaining a position as a _____

   with your agency? _____

   _____

2. Do you have any examinations for this type of work open now? _____

   If yes, how may I apply and what is involved? _____

   _____

   If no, when might an examination be held? _____

3. Do you sometimes employ qualified people on a temporary or part-time basis? _____

4. What is the starting salary/salary range for the type of position that I am interested in? _____

5. For what types of positions do you do most of your hiring? _____

   _____

6. Is there a promotion procedure that might help me to advance if I start at a low or entry-level position? _____

   _____

7. Can you make any suggestions about other government agencies where there is a good possibility that people with my type of qualifications will be hired in the near future? _____

   _____

Worksheet: Learning About Possible Political Job Openings

Using the format supplied below, call the office of a political candidate for a major elective office—federal, state, or city. Those elected to minor offices are seldom able to hire much staff, and the few positions they can fill usually go to family, relatives, or close friends. You will be seeking a volunteer slot, and full- or part-time workers are usually welcomed. Pick a candidate of your own political party or one whose stands on many issues are the same as yours.

Name of candidate _____

Office being sought _____

Campaign headquarters address _____

Phone _____

Candidate's home address _____

Phone _____

Name of campaign manager _____

Name and title of contact at campaign headquarters _____

_____

Results/follow-up _____

_____

_____

_____

_____

_____

Applications and Resumes: Your "Paper" Qualifications

If you have a well-prepared resume, you may be tempted to refuse or at least object when you are handed an application form to complete. All the information it asks for is already in your resume.

Don't give in to the temptation. Complete all applications cheerfully. Each organization to which you apply will want you to complete its particular form for several good reasons.

In the first place, almost every person's resume is organized somewhat differently. A filled-out application is a convenience to experienced interviewers in locating items that they want to check or ask about. They know just where to look for your social security number, your current address, or tools or machines you can use.

Second, many people forget or neglect to include in their resume information that is important to different organizations. Finally, having all applicants complete the organization's standard form is a filing convenience—it is easier to locate in the files than resumes.

Prepare a Resume

A resume is a written description of a person's education, experience, and any other job-related qualifications, plus identifying information.

In addition to using resumes for hand-carrying or mailing responses to box-number ads, they come in handy because you are able quickly and easily to transfer information from them to application forms. Further, if you have prepared fairly long, detailed descriptions of your experience and you find that an application form provides too little space, you can refer the employer to your resume by attaching it to the application.

If you are just out of school, have had no job experience, did little or nothing outstanding in extracurricular activities, or never achieved leadership capacity, you don't need to prepare a resume. On the other hand, if you are fresh out of school and served in a leadership role in school activities, scouting, 4-H programs, sports, and youth clubs, describe these in a short summary. Make copies and attach one to each application that does not have an appropriate space for reporting such achievements and recognition.

Resumes are of greatest value to people who have held many different types of jobs and those persons who have held unusually complex jobs. Managers, executives, researchers, scientists, and technicians doing complicated work find that a well-thought-out resume is essential. Few application forms provide sufficient space for all the details these people need to present to describe their experience and capabilities.

How to Organize Your Resume

All resumes ought to begin with an objective (the type of position desired), name, address, and other identifying information. Next education is described. Then the experience portion can be organized in one of three ways: (1) chronologically, with each job described in the order held; (2) functionally, with experience summarized by type of work experience instead of according to dates; and (3) combination, with a functional summary at the beginning followed by a chronological description of each job held.

The chronological resume is the most common and is essentially the same as most application forms in terms of arrangement. Organizing your qualifications in this format is fine if your work history is short and/or uncomplicated. A functionally organized resume will be to your advantage when you have had a number of different types of jobs and you want to pull parts of them together to show an accumulation of certain types of experience. The combination has the advantages but not the disadvantages of the other two.

With each of the three experience arrangements, you begin your resume with the same two lead-in sections: "Personal Data," and "Education."

Personal data

Put your name, address, and phone number(s) at the top. Do not indicate the type of job you are applying for but leave some space for it. After you have copies made, fill in the space with the name of the particular job you are applying for as advertised or otherwise made known to you.

Don't list any personal data that might be to your disadvantage. For example, don't indicate your date of birth. If you are a woman with small children, make no mention of them. (Many such women have to lose time from the job when children are out of school for holidays or are sick.) If you have a physical handicap, don't list it. Your first objective is to get an interview and an opportunity to sell yourself. Don't cut yourself out before you get a turn at bat.

Other personal information is optional. Few interviewers have any faith in items such as describing the status of your health. Forget about hobbies. Taking space on an employment application or resume to relate that you are into archery, pottery, fishing, or knitting, for example, is inappropriate. If the interviewer wants to know about the subject, you will be asked and will then provide some fuel for the conversation.

Education

The less experience you have had, the more important it is to provide detailed information about your education. If you were just recently graduated or have been out of school for only a short time, list all the courses you completed that have a bearing on the job. Mention any honors you received and extracurricular accomplishments. If you are older, cut your education section down to the bare essentials.

How to Describe Your Experience
The chronological resume

In preparing chronological resumes, you start with your present or most recent job and work backward to your first important employment. In addition to describing your regular duties, be sure to include mention of any extra things that you did. For example, you might have trained or helped to train new employees, an assignment that was not part of your formal duties. Perhaps you came up with ideas that your boss approved and that were adopted for improving efficiency or getting better quality. The little extras can help put you ahead of your competitors.

For each job, include the name, title, and phone number of your boss (or someone else who will speak more favorably of you if you and your boss didn't get along). Include the date you started each job and when you left if you are no longer there. Some people insert the beginning and final salary for each job, but final salary is sufficient for most purposes.

You can include some personal references (friends or your religious leader) if you so desire, but few employers will pay much attention to them. They know that applicants will list only people who will speak well of them and who may have only a little knowledge of the individual's ability to perform well on the job. Of course, if you are just out of school and have had little or no experience, list a few, such as a teacher, coach, counselor, or prominent person in the community. Be sure to ask these people for permission to use their names. They will then be better prepared to endorse you if they get a call.

If you are in a professional field, you will need to spend whatever time and effort is required to provide detailed and specific information about research you have done, honors bestowed, articles published, and any major managerial or corporate accomplishments that could swing a hiring decision in your favor.

The functional resume

In a purely functional resume, use no dates of employment. Instead, provide a fairly detailed summary for each type of job or task that you have performed for one or more employers.

By doing this, experience gained in many different jobs can be pulled together into summary statements that may be much more impressive than when the experience is scattered among many of the jobs in a chronological resume.

Suppose, for example, that a person has had three secretarial jobs, has worked as a cashier in a restaurant, and has been a salesclerk in a retail store. The job being applied for is purchasing assistant for a large company. Assume also that the individual applying has had a little bit of purchasing experience in some of those previous jobs. Most secretaries buy office supplies, and many make recommendations on the acquisition of some types of equipment and furnishings. An experienced salesclerk in a small store may work closely with the manager in merchandise buying. The cashiering experience may have nothing to contribute, but the other jobs, cumulatively, may show a lot of buying knowhow. In this case, grouping the total experience into functional blocks, such as purchasing, secretarial, and cashiering, is the best way to organize the experience. The relevant experience for the purchasing assistant job might be written up something like this.

> More than three years of experience in different positions, developing sources for purchasing, interviewing sales representatives, checking the quality and satisfaction with other purchasers, negotiating prices and discounts, preparing purchase orders, placing orders, and checking incoming shipments against orders.

Combined chronological and functional

With this type of resume, one or more functional statements combining selected experiences taken from different jobs are set forth after the personal data and education. The functional statements are then followed by a chronological listing and description of each current and previous job.

The combination resume involves more time and work than the chronological or purely functional ones not only to prepare but to revise. However, the combination version is best, because it serves to highlight experiences that are relevant to the job you are targeting, and it has the advantage, from the reviewer's point of view, of also including a chronology of positions held.

For maximum effectiveness the functional portion should fit the requirements of the job being sought as perfectly as possible. If practical, call and ask about the job in some detail before preparing and submitting a resume.

Examples of each type of resume have been provided at the end of this chapter.

Do's and Don'ts

There isn't much you can do wrong in listing the facts about your education, but here are some important points about describing your work experience.

Not too short or too long   An overly long or too complicated resume can mark you as a tiresome bore. Just as you can talk so much about yourself in an interview that you talk yourself out of the job, you can write too much. Reviewers of a resume are annoyed to have to wade through pages and pages of trivial information. How long is too long? There is no fixed rule. Many people who have had a half-lifetime or more of experience have a lot of good ground to cover. Nevertheless, anything more than a total of five pages is probably dangerous. No more than three pages is a sound general rule.

A resume can be only one page if your experience has been fairly limited and if you can do justice to yourself in that much space. A half page is undoubtedly too little because at least half of it will be needed for your personal data and education.

If you have had a lot of different jobs, but some of them have absolutely no bearing on the one you are applying for, you can describe the unrelated ones briefly. Then write fully and in detail about the job or jobs that you feel best qualify you for the one that you are going after.

Facts and important details   People who read a lot of resumes appreciate most the ones that provide facts and important details. Resumes containing a lot of generalities but leaving out needed data are often cast aside. Here are some of the facts people want and need:

- Your name, home address, and telephone numbers

- Your job title, your employer's name and address, and the dates of employment for all former jobs

- Degrees you have earned, where you earned them, and dates of attendance

Don't exaggerate   While some employers don't verify education, previous salaries, or job experience, many do. If you are caught lying in your resume, your chances are lost immediately. If you are hired by a government agency and the information in your resume or application is found to have been falsified, you can be in big trouble. You not only can be dismissed, but criminal charges can be brought against you.

Make it professional

No matter what job you are seeking, make your resume a professional presentation. It represents you. In many cases you won't be there when it is received, so it will carry full responsibility for getting you into the next stage—the interview.

Have your resume professionally typed if you can. Be sure your spelling and grammar are perfect. If you are not very good at those subjects, get help from a friend or relative who is, but go to whatever lengths to get it perfect.

When you have copies of your resume made, keep the original for yourself. When you go to a copy service, ask them first to make only one copy. Examine it closely for black spots and smudges. If you find some, go elsewhere. Their sloppiness will make you look bad, not them.

Special Problems

Protect your present job

You may want to withhold giving out any identifying information about your present job unless you have already given notice to, or been given notice by, your current employer. The problem here is that your present job may have provided you with the best experience you have had to date, especially in terms of qualifying for the kind of new and better job you want to get through your resume or application. You can take some steps to protect your position.

Omit specifics about your present job. When filling in application forms handed to you by prospective employers or when developing a resume, complete the description of your present duties but omit the name, address, and phone number of your present employer. In the space provided on an application or in your resume, write "supplied on request." This gives you better protection than supplying all the information and adding the word confidential, which sometimes is inadvertently overlooked.

Use the functional format in preparing your resume. In this type of resume you don't list any specific jobs or employers. Provide only a summary statement covering each of the various types of functions you have performed, grouping or consolidating them by functions. While this approach may not be as desirable from the prospective employer's standpoint, it can provide the privacy you may temporarily need about your present job.

Include a strong statement that your present employer is not to be contacted at the preliminary stage of negotiations. This requires more than just indicating "confidential" with respect to your current employment. Use a statement something like this: "It is very important that no contact be made with my present employer before I am notified, at which time I will be pleased to supply names and phone numbers as requested. Thank you." When you are notified, the job should be almost yours.

Minimize bad references

Always strive as hard as is possible to build a good reputation with every employer you work for. This not only means performing your work well, but it also means becoming known as a person who is easy to supervise and easy to get along with in relation to other employees, customers, and suppliers.

Bad references can be the result of many failures or misdeeds. Being chronically late or frequently absent (even for good reasons) can be damaging. Carelessness and a sloppy appearance earn a bad reputation. Dishonesty, lying, or stealing are murderous to a fired employee's chances for good future jobs. Of all the bad reports on prospective employees, the most frequent one is, "Doesn't get along well with others." What can you do to minimize the fact that you have left a "dirty nest" somewhere? If prospective employers check you out thoroughly, you could have a tough time. However, here are some things you can do to help your situation.

Go to the person you think will give you bad marks and have a private talk about it. Don't just phone. It is harder for the other person to maintain a negative position against you when you are face-to-face. Go to the person's office and suggest the two of you go for coffee. Don't rehash the problems. Begin by establishing a pleasant, relaxed relationship, if you can. Exchange a few pleasantries, ask about the person's family, and smile. Lead up to what you came to talk about by speaking enthusiastically of the new job you hope to get. Then, with the stage set, pop the question. Plan what you are going to say and practice a few times so it will come out smoothly. In planning your request, avoid asking the person if in effect he or she will lie for you. Put your request in vague, general terms. Here are a few examples that may help you:

This opportunity means everything to me, and I'd like to use your name as a reference. Will you help me?

This job I am after will give me a whole new start. If I give your name as a reference, will you help me get it?

I would like to give your name as a reference, but I thought I ought to ask your permission first. Will it be okay? I really need this job.

When approached in this manner, some people will do a complete turnaround and give you a better reference than they might have. Others will tell you they won't volunteer any negative information and, if they are pressed, will put you in as favorable a light as possible. In a few instances, the person may take a negative position in the matter, but you won't have lost anything by trying.

Put down as a reference the name of someone other than the boss you believe will torpedo your future job opportunities. If you have had more than one boss while employed by the organization, list the boss you feel will give you the best recommendation. If you do this, be sure to tell the person whose name you are listing so he or she doesn't refer the call to the boss whose negative evaluation you are trying to escape.

If the job lasted only for a very short time, some people simply don't report it on applications or resumes. In the case of jobs that have lasted only a few weeks or a month, many applicants will assume that the experience was too short to matter and will simply not report it. This is done in spite of the fact that most applications carry the instruction to list all employment and account for any periods of unemployment. If you are convinced some brief job would be negative and you omit it, don't cover it up with a false statement. Just leave it out. Most interviewers either won't pick it up or will ignore small disconnections in the continuity of your employment history.

If the employment period was substantial and you are concerned about a negative reference, report the position but omit reference information. If you can list an alternative boss at the same place who will speak well of you, fine. Otherwise, use a statement like this: "It is very important that no contact be made with employers before I am notified, at which time I will be pleased to supply names and phone numbers." Then if you get the interview and a chance to sell yourself, you can soften the effect of the bad reference by giving your side of the story first.

Police records

Many applications contain this type of statement: "If you have ever been arrested or convicted of any crime other than minor traffic violations, list nature of offense, court dates, fines and/or sentences, and whether you are currently on parole."

There is no reason to mention a police record on your resume, and you may be able to get away with ignoring the item on the application forms most companies provide. However, if you are completing an application for government and many other positions, failure to report a police record as required will be discovered, and you can find yourself in violation of the law as well as not getting the job or losing it if the omission is discovered later. Leaving the item blank on application forms for private companies may at least get you to the interview stage. There you will probably be asked why you failed to answer the item. You can give the best explanation available to you, hoping it won't bar you from getting the job. Don't apply for any job in which you would be faced with the temptation to commit another crime, if you have a specific weakness. A counselor can help you avoid problems and find the best kind of situation.

Job-hoppers

A job-hopper is a person who quits or is let go after short periods of employment. This kind of record is a serious negative. Put yourself in the place of a prospective employer. Employee turnover is a costly nuisance. When an employee quits or has to be fired, the recruitment process has to start all over again. Time and production may be lost, and a new person will need to be trained. If you were the employer and received a resume that showed that an applicant had changed jobs frequently, you might not want to bother interviewing the person to find out why.

What if you, as an applicant, already have a record indicating you are a job-hopper? You can't change the record, but you can try to minimize its negative effect on you and thereby at least improve your chances of getting interviews.

For example, you can prepare a functional resume. This won't show dates or lengths of employment. Or you can work up a chronological or combination resume and list in chronological order only the jobs you held for more than short periods of time. Then add a separate section at the end under the heading "Temporary Employment." List all the short-term jobs there, including the dates. Putting these quick in-and-out jobs under the heading "Temporary Employment" establishes, by implication, that those jobs were offered and accepted with the understanding they were to last only for a short time.

Complete applications the same way. When you come to the part asking for your employment history, print in bold letters: "See resume, attached." Then hope for the best. Many employers will accept this, and if the interviewer isn't very sharp, you will have a good chance of getting away with it.

Prevention is the only real cure, however. If you have been hopping around from job to job, settle down, and in time, your period of instability will drift into the background.

Reasons for having left jobs

Most applications ask the reason you left each previous position. Be careful how you answer. Employers are looking for negative implications in reasons that may be perfectly legitimate. Reasons to be avoided include "personality conflict," "job was boring," "work was too hard," "health problems," "supervisor too strict," "people were nasty."

You must not give a false reason, but if you have left most of your previous jobs for a combination of reasons, which is the case with most people, you can give the least damaging reason. The space provided is always limited, and you have no obligation to write an essay.

"To return to school" is probably the most acceptable reason when there is a long lapse of time between two jobs. "Better salary" is an adequate reason, provided the facts show that you did get a significant raise as a result of making the move. "Better opportunity" and "opportunity for advancement" are both good and are used frequently, but be ready to explain what you mean.

Physical handicaps or health problems

As indicated previously, there is no value in claiming excellent health in a resume. Most applications won't require you to report on the state of your health for the same reason. However, many applications call for you to indicate any physical handicaps. If you have an obvious physical handicap, such as blindness, need to use crutches, a walker, wheelchair, or artificial arm, alert interviewers in advance. Don't describe your handicap in your resume, and avoid listing it in applications. Instead, alert interviewers in advance by phone. When you are talking, casually mention your handicap, but don't make a big deal of it. Say something like: "Incidentally, I make up with efficiency and hard work for the fact that I have (a hearing aid, artificial left arm, a wheelchair). I wanted you to know about that in advance."

Also, if you have an obvious handicap, see if there is a Hire-the-Handicapped program in your area. Check with the local state employment service. You may find it to your advantage to have a professional call and do a selling job for you. He or she may begin by asking the employer how many handicapped persons are already in its employ, which frequently will be far too few. If so, it provides a springboard for motivating the interviewer to give you a chance to show what you can do.

Mass Mailing Resumes

For individuals whose job skills are not scarce, sending out hundreds of resumes is mostly fruitless. However, if you can afford it and are the gambling type, go ahead. Once in a great while such a mailed resume hits at exactly the right time—when someone has quit suddenly without notice, resulting in a severe emergency. There may not be any qualified applicants on file, and there could be too little time to go through the usual recruitment process. Again, it is a rare occurrence.

Make copies of your resume and cover letter. For just a few copies of a resume, machine copies cost less than printing. For larger quantities, such as a hundred or more, printing is normally less expensive and can be vastly better. If you can afford it, pay extra for a good grade of bond paper, but avoid spending a lot of money for typesetting and graphics. An expensively designed and decorated resume destroys the personal, one-on-one effect you ought to try to maintain even in a mass mailing. Professional quality typing is fine.

If you can afford to spend something extra, buy 9 × 12-inch envelopes, in white, with your name and address printed in the upper left corner. Mailed in the large envelope, your standard 8½ × 11-inch resume will lie flat and not have to be folded.

Mailing lists   If you are sending out a very large quantity, see a company that rents specialized mailing lists. Look in the yellow pages. Visit one or two; tell them the kinds of organizations you have in mind, and see what they can do for you. You won't get the list. You will have to give them your envelopes, cover letters, and resume copies. They will address your envelopes, put addresses and salutations on the cover letters, insert, and mail for you. This is an enormous timesaver. Take advantage of it if you can.

If for some reason you choose not to go that route, you can work up your own mailing list. Larger cities have business directories available at the local chamber of commerce or public library. The yellow pages are a good source because you can find companies grouped by the type of product or service. The yellow pages do not include zip codes, but directories are available at your local library and at post offices.

Cover letters   You need a cover letter for each resume you send. If you are going to do a big mailing, send the same letter to all your addresses, but do not personalize addresses and salutations. Personalized letters are more effective, but the problem is cost. If you are sending out a modest quantity, fewer than 50, you ought to be able to do the job yourself. Obtain names and titles by calling each target organization. Simply say, "I want to write a letter to your company (president, manager, owner, personnel director, employment manager). Would you please give me the correct spelling and title?"

A general type of cover letter you can use to send a resume to a box number or employment office in response to a classified ad is presented at the end of this chapter. You will also see an example of a personalized letter you might use in trying to get your resume to a specific top executive. Always include a reason you would like to work for the organization. If you have any knowledge of the individual to whom you are writing, make the most of it. For example, you may have read in the paper recently about a speech the person made. Perhaps you have a good friend who works for the organization and have permission to use her or his name. If so, write something like: "Lori Morgan, who works in your research department, has suggested I write to you personally about my interest in working for you and your company."

Friends like to help.   Job seekers often get fine results through a modest circle of friends and relatives. Those friends and relatives who are employed, or who were employed for a considerable time, nearly always enjoy helping close ones get located.

Employers like being helped.   Of even greater importance in this regard is the premium most employers place on the value of recommendations. In the first place they avoid the time and expense involved in recruiting good candidates. Moreover, employers learn to be very appreciative of the process because they find that no employees in their right minds would go on record recommending the hiring of a stupid, difficult, unreliable person. Even if such a candidate got by a perfunctory screening, the truth would soon out.

Time and effort would have been wasted, and the employer would be back to square one. Because bad recommendations happen so very rarely, or simply never happen, the employee-recommended method is continually growing in use everywhere.

So, make up some extra resumes, see that all your friends and favorite work-experienced relatives get a copy with a warm personal note. Identify your area(s) of interest, and outline your qualifications in the note. You'll double the response if you also take a minute to call each of your new "eyes and ears."

Worksheet: Recording Details for Use in Preparing Your Resume

Using the format below, prepare a detailed record of information that you will want to be sure to include in your resume, whether chronological, functional, or combination. Doing this thoroughly and thoughtfully will save time when you write the resume and will help you avoid overlooking essential data.

Objective: _____

_____

Education:

Name of school/training program _____

Address and telephone _____

Year(s) graduated or attended _____

Degree received _____

Name of school/training program _____

Address and telephone _____

Year(s) graduated or attended _____

Degree received _____

Name of school/training program _____

Address and telephone _____

Year(s) graduated or attended _____

Degree received _____

Work Experience:

Employer's name _____

Address and telephone _____

Supervisor's name _____

Dates employed _____

Starting, ending pay _____

Job title _____

List of duties _____

_____

_____

_____

Employer's name _____

Address and telephone _____

Supervisor's name _____

Dates employed _____

Starting, ending pay _____

Job title _____

List of duties _____

_____

_____

Employer's name _____

Address and telephone _____

Supervisor's name _____

Dates employed _____

Starting, ending pay _____

Job title _____

List of duties _____

_____

_____

Special Accomplishments, Awards, and Qualifications:

_____

_____

_____

_____

_____

Example: Chronological Resume

John D. Smith
115 Elm Street, Apt. 214
Tower, Indiana 11111
Phone: 555-2222

Objective:	A position as an air-conditioning/heating mechanic.
Education:	Great Lakes Naval Training Station, North Chicago, Illinois, eight-month Electricians' Mate Training Course, 1982.
	Westinghouse Technical School, Elkhart, Indiana, six-week course in air-conditioning mechanics, 1981.
	Tower High School, Tower, Indiana, 1976–80.

Work Experience:

May 1986 to present	Norton Construction Company, Tower, Indiana Installation Mechanic Installed ductwork and wiring for air conditioners made by various manufacturers, such as GE, Trane, Fedders, Westinghouse, and Luxaire. This experience included pretesting of installed units for proper operation, use of test equipment to troubleshoot for defects, and arranging for and supervising any needed warranty work to get problems taken care of at time of installation.
October 1983 to May 1986	Bellweather Apartment Complex, Tower, Indiana Stationary Engineer In charge of all utilities, including water, heating, and air conditioning. This building contained 256 units, each with one or more GE window air conditioners, five to seven years old. Duties included ordering and stocking spare parts, hiring additional mechanical help as needed, and doing minor electrical, carpentry, and masonry work.
June 1982 to September 1983	U.S. Navy, Cruisers and Destroyers Electricians' Mate Worked on maintenance and operation of shipboard boilers and oil- and gas-fired furnaces, doing troubleshooting, repair, or replacement of all components. Had responsibility for maintaining proper temperatures and pressures under all conditions, both in port and at sea.
	References provided upon request.

Example: Functional Resume

John D. Smith
115 Elm Street, Apt. 214
Tower, Indiana 11111
Phone: 555-2222

Objective: A position as an air-conditioning/heating mechanic.

Experience:

Residential Air Conditioning

Total of two years' experience in new-house construction involving the installation of ductwork and wiring for air conditioners manufactured by GE, Trane, Fedders, Westinghouse, and Luxaire. This experience has included pretesting of installed units for proper operation, the use of test equipment to troubleshoot for defects, and arranging for and supervising any needed warranty work to get problems taken care of at time of installation. Three years' experience in general building maintenance, which included mechanical servicing of window-unit air conditioners.

Furnace and Boiler Repair

A combined total of almost three years in the maintenance and repair of boilers and oil- and gas-fired furnaces. This included preventive maintenance as well as troubleshooting, repair or replacement of thermostats, zone switches, blower units, igniters, fire cores, and flue systems. Boiler maintenance included repair of all types of pressure and temperature gauges, feeder lines, distribution boxes, and monitoring devices.

Other

Experienced in small appliance repair, including kitchen items, space heaters, clocks, hair driers, and small electric motors and compressors.

Education:

Great Lakes Naval Training Station, North Chicago, Illinois, eight-month Electricians' Mate Training Course, 1982.

Westinghouse Technical School, Elkhart, Indiana, six-week course in air-conditioning mechanics, 1981.

Tower High School, Tower, Indiana, 1976–80.

Example: Combination Chronological and Functional Resume

John D. Smith
115 Elm Street, Apt. 214
Tower, Indiana 11111
Phone: 555-2222

Objective:	A position as an air-conditioning/heating mechanic.
Residential Air Conditioning	Two years' experience in new-house construction involving the installation of ductwork and wiring for air conditioners manufactured by Trane, GE, Fedders, Westinghouse, and Luxaire. Also tested and repaired installed units.
Furnace and Boiler Repair	Combined total of almost three years in the maintenance and repair of boilers and oil- and gas-fired furnaces.
Other	Experienced in small appliance repair, including kitchen items, space heaters, clocks, hair driers, and small electric motors and compressors.
	******
Experience:	Installation Mechanic, Norton Construction Company, 114 W. Oakton St., Tower, Indiana 10101. Supervisor, John Madigan. May 1986 to present.
	Stationary Engineer, Bellweather Apartment Complex, 2121 Ogden Ave., Tower, Indiana 10102. Supervisor, Norma L. Jones. October 1983 to May 1986.
Education:	Great Lakes Naval Training Station, North Chicago, Illinois, eight-month Electricians' Mate Training Course, 1982. Westinghouse Technical School, Elkhart, Indiana, six-week course in air-conditioning mechanics, 1981. Tower High School, Tower, Indiana, 1976–80.

Worksheet: Making Up Your Resume

Following the suggestions in the chapter, make a rough draft of your resume. Ask a friend to read it and make suggestions as well. Then rewrite and improve any parts that need changing and fill them in below. Use a second sheet if necessary.

Name _____

Address _____

_____

_____

Phone _____

Objective _____

_____

_____

Educational Background

(List most recent schooling first.)   (Courses and/or specialization)

_____   _____

_____   _____

_____   _____

_____   _____

_____   _____

_____   _____

_____   _____

_____   _____

_____   _____

_____   _____

Work Experience

(List most recent job titles, company names, and addresses first)

(Job descriptions and accomplishments)

_____   _____

_____   _____

_____   _____

_____   _____

_____   _____

_____   _____

_____   _____

_____   _____

_____   _____

_____   _____

_____   _____

_____   _____

_____   _____

_____   _____

_____   _____

_____   _____

_____   _____

_____   _____

_____   _____

Worksheet: Mailing List for Sending Resumes

Using the spaces below, record the names and/or titles of key people and organizations to whom you plan to send resumes and cover letters.

Name/Title Key Person	Organization/Department	Address and Phone No.

Worksheet: Application Record for Follow-up Purposes

Here is a convenient format for keeping track of applications or resumes you have submitted so that you can follow-up on those that appear attractive and that you have reason to believe hold future possibilities for you.

Organization _____

Name and title of person talked with _____

Date of conversation _____

Results/follow-up _____

_____

_____

Interview date _____

Results from interview _____

_____

_____

Organization _____

Name and title of person talked with _____

Date of conversation _____

Results/follow-up _____

_____

_____

Interview date _____

Results from interview _____

_____

_____

Organization _____

Name and title of person talked with _____

Date of conversation _____

Results/follow-up _____

_____

_____

Interview date _____

Results from interview _____

_____

_____

Organization _____

Name and title of person talked with _____

Date of conversation _____

Results/follow-up _____

_____

_____

Interview date _____

Results from interview _____

_____

_____

Organization _____

Name and title of person talked with _____

Date of conversation _____

Results/follow-up _____

_____

_____

Interview date _____

Results from interview _____

_____

_____

Example: General Cover Letter

599 Douglas Drive
Kansas City, Missouri 64112
November 8, 19___

Personnel Director
Box 16072
4600 Madison Avenue
Kansas City, Missouri 64111

Dear Sir/Madam:

The resume that I have attached describes my two years' experience as a receptionist for the Macklin Corporation and other related paid positions I have held.

As you can see, I am also a qualified typist and have had a variety of clerical experience, including simple bookkeeping, and I am very willing to perform extra duties at times when there are few clients or visitors.

In addition, for a period of three years I worked two days a week as a volunteer visitors' hours receptionist for the Melville County General Hospital under the supervision of Mrs. Elaine Sutherland, Senior Representative, American Red Cross Volunteer Services. She can be reached at the hospital for verification at 616-1111.

My phone number is 555-4616, and I hope you'll be able to have someone give me a call. I can be there for an interview almost anytime and can report for duty on short notice.

Thank you.

Sincerely,

Lisa Gonzalez

Example: Personalized Cover Letter

602 Hadley Avenue
Kettering, Ohio 45314
September 9, 19___

Mr. John D. Eddington, President
Eddington Trucking Corporation
1111 Main Avenue
Dayton, Ohio 45419

Dear Mr. Eddington:

I read in the paper yesterday that your company is starting an expansion program and that you've ordered a new fleet of GM tractors and trailers. Harry Brownell, who I understand has been driving for you for almost 20 years, suggested that I write this letter to you. He says ETC is the best company in this area to work for, and I'd like to be a part of your organization.

As you can see from my attached resume, I have had five years' experience driving for Durham Brothers' Trucking Company in Fairborn. I would bring to your company the valuable practical experience I have gained from driving GM tractors and trailers there.

My phone number is 555-7611, and I hope you'll be able to have someone give me a call. I can be there for an interview almost anytime and can report for duty on short notice.

Thank you.

Sincerely,

Jim Finelli

Worksheet: Draft of Cover Letter To Be Sent with Resume

In the spaces below, compose a draft of a cover letter to be sent with your resume to the organizations on your mailing list. Do at least one revision. Do more than one draft if needed until you are satisfied.

Your Address _____

_____

_____

Telephone: Home_____

Name and Title _____

Organization _____

Department _____

Street _____

City/State/Zip _____

Dear _____:

_____

_____

_____

_____

_____

_____

_____

_____

_____

_____

_____

_____

_____

_____

_____

_____

Sincerely,

_____

The Interview: A Performance

Three main factors affect whether you will get the job for which you apply. Each has to do with how well you stack up in relation to your competitors, who are also trying their best to succeed in the same categories:

1. Your paper qualifications—the content and appearance of your application and/or resume

2. What your references have to say about your performance and behavior while you worked for them

3. How you perform in your interview(s)

Ideally, you will be the best candidate on the basis of all three factors. In most cases when applicants are called in for an interview, they are considered qualified on the basis of their resume or application. You can't do much about what your references say about you. You are left with your final turn at bat: your chance to deliver a stellar performance when you are interviewed. If you blow the interview, you can't expect to get the job.

Charm and Confidence

If experience has told you that you don't naturally perform well in these situations, you are not alone. How many people are just naturally charming, relaxed, interesting, and enjoyable for almost anyone to talk with? As a vital part of being excellent conversationalists, some are also alert, attentive listeners. For these few fortunate people, interviews are no problem. They may not get the job every time, but it is never because they don't take first prize in the interview portion of the hiring process.

Most of us, on the other hand, are not naturally relaxed charmers. If you have found that you don't perform as well in interviews as you would like, then it will pay for you to work to improve. You need to learn to make the most of whatever acting ability you have, because in being interviewed you are going to be relying upon learned behavior.

Performing well in an interview does not mean trying to be an entirely different person from what you are. It means that you must identify any handicaps you have in competing with other applicants and eliminate or minimize them. Handicaps that can be overcome include excessive nervousness, abnormal amount of shyness, or simply a dull personality. To do something about your weaknesses, you must first recognize them and face them honestly. Then you can strengthen them through preparation, including rehearsing.

Rehearse To Develop Confidence

If you find you are uptight about being interviewed for jobs and you really want to come off with top honors in relation to other applicants, you will need to devote some time and effort to rehearsing.

Rehearsing will help you get much better organized so that you can answer expected questions correctly and confidently, without the stumbling and fumbling that you might otherwise go through. Being a little nervous at the start of your interviews is nothing to be concerned about. A little nervousness can stimulate your mind to think better.

However, rehearsing will cut back substantially on excessive nervousness.

You will need someone who is willing to work with you. The best person is a close friend or relative who has been through a number of job interviews. If this person is also planning to start looking for a better job, both of you can practice changing roles as the interviewer and as the applicant.

Find a private place, such as a living room, dining room, or family room, and get rid of everyone but the two of you. Don't permit any spectators or jokesters to observe or listen in.

Role play   Use a dining room table or a card table as a desk. Have the person who is playing the role of interviewer sit behind it, with some papers lying on the surface to add a touch of realism. You will need a chair for each person, one behind the "desk" and one alongside of it.

Work together to prepare a list of questions for the interviewer to ask. The list can be simple, but make it as realistic as you can. The list does not have to be followed in order. Which questions the interviewer will ask will depend sometimes on the previous answers given and sometimes on the interviewer's judgment and preferences. See the worksheet at the end of the chapter for a list of questions interviewers often ask.

Relax   *Be likable!* There is no need to be grim in doing these rehearsals, and you will feel more relaxed as you go through the process at least several times. Don't treat the rehearsals too lightly. It is a serious procedure, and if you and your partner practice in a businesslike but friendly way, it will have a highly favorable effect on your interview performance.

When you have the stage set and any props in place, take the role of the applicant. Leave the room. Reenter with an envelope in your hand containing a copy of your resume. The friend who is performing the part of the interviewer should rise from the chair behind the desk, offer a hand, give her or his name, get yours, determine which position you are applying for, and invite you to have a seat. This is what typically happens in real-life situations.

Then the interviewer should take a minute or two to put you at ease with some friendly small talk. Next, an interviewer will usually ask for your resume or application. After reviewing it briefly, there may be specific questions. Or sometimes the interviewer will just say, "Tell me something about yourself."

As explained previously, interviewers will usually want you to tell them things about your past that are already available to them in your resume or application. They do this for at least two good reasons. First, they may want more detail than you have furnished in writing, particularly if they have only a short-form application and not a more detailed one or a resume. Second, interviewers want to hear you talk for a while. This gives them some basis for forming certain judgments about your attitudes, personality, and your ability to talk in an organized way.

Be prepared to tell your background in your own words

When you respond to questions or invitations to talk about yourself as you are rehearsing, don't keep cutting your responses shorter and shorter. You may feel it is senseless to tell your partner the same things over and over, but it is not. This is what rehearsals are all about: repeating your lines until you know them well and can deliver them confidently.

Each time you go through a rehearsal as the interviewee you will find that you are responding more smoothly and confidently. That may cause you to wonder if you will do nearly so well in a real interview situation. You will do even better. When you get into an actual interview, you will talk with more vitality and say everything with a degree of self-assurance that is bound to go over well.

Confirm Your Interview Appointments

Confirming appointments is a standard business practice and will indicate to the other party that you are a knowledgeable and orderly person. You may also want to be sure you have the correct address of the company and get any travel directions you may need. Also, if there is a delay in the time of the interview or if the date of the appointment has changed, you will avoid a needless trip. Or perhaps another interviewer will take the appointment. Say something like this: "My name is Randy Fisher. I have an appointment scheduled for Friday at three o'clock with Ms./Mr. Cohen, and I want to make sure it is still convenient for her/him."

That Important First Impression

As previously emphasized, in getting a good job you always have competition. You need to win over other applicants in as many of the three categories as you possibly can. But if you do well in your interviews, you will often get the job over other applicants who were somewhat better in the other two categories.

Start off by making a great first impression. The well-trained person who performs the interviewing function understands and accepts the fact that many applicants will show some signs of nervousness. This is why you can expect them to start by talking about the weather, a recent news event, or some other neutral topic. They like to feel they are succeeding, so you will do well to fit right in and contribute to the small talk. Most interviewers are almost bound to have some mental reservation when an applicant continues to sit there, obviously tense and largely uncommunicative. Rehearsing can help you avoid feeling ridiculous and will help you to develop the kind of relaxed relationship with the interviewer that will help your cause.

Four additional keys to making a good first impression are discussed next.

Punctuality

Most interviewers work on a tight schedule. They have a strong negative reaction to applicants who fail to show up on time for their interviews. Of course it doesn't seem to bother a lot of interviewers to keep applicants waiting. If you must be late, call ahead and explain your problem. A good excuse helps a little, but a tardy applicant starts off the interview with at least one strike, regardless of the reason for the lateness.

Appropriate dress

Interviewers' judgments of you are always affected by the way you dress. It is a mistake to be overdressed or too informally dressed for the position you are seeking. Wear the best-looking work clothes you have and be prepared to go to work immediately if you are available. For office jobs, dress conservatively with a touch of flair. For example, a woman should wear conservative clothes with perhaps a little different styling or a handsome accessory. A man should wear conservative colors. You will usually make a better impression if the style is modern or if your shirt or tie is a cut above the ordinary. If you have a doubt as to how to dress, visit the place a day ahead of time and look around to see how the people who are doing your kind of work are dressed. If you have been out of work for awhile and your wardrobe is not what you would like it to be, don't despair. Borrow from friends, visit resale and thrift shops, and put together the most appropriate outfit you can. Then go out and put your show on the road.

Personal grooming

If you have never been in the employment business, it might be hard for you to imagine how important good grooming is. Make every effort to be neat, clean, and modestly dressed. A first impression can be the deciding factor, so be sure to avoid extremes in dress, too much perfume, cologne, or makeup, or wildly faddish hairstyles.

Self-confidence

Continued nervousness beyond the first several minutes of an interview is a definite negative to some interviewers. Even if the interviewer is tolerant and understanding of it, the condition prevents you from responding to him or her as well as you might. It can also falsely lead the interviewer to believe you are such a jittery person that you might do poor work. Self-confidence is not the same as cockiness or arrogance. What you need to work toward is confidence that you have ready the answers you will need and that you can deliver them in a friendly, self-assured manner.

The Interview: Two-Way Communication

Whether you are to see someone on the employment office staff or the person who would be your boss if you get the job, interviews need to be two-way affairs. The interviewer will want certain things from you, and you need to size up the situation to decide if you want the job. Assuming, for example, that you have outstanding qualifications for the better job that you are seeking, you may not want to take just any job that is offered.

In the interviews be alert and sensitive to the manner and attitudes of the people who represent the management of the organization. In many cases, the way they talk and act reflects the attitudes and behavior predominant throughout the organization. So even if you get an offer, you must ask yourself if this is a place where you would really like to work.

The question is important, because if you accept the offer, you will have to give up the job you presently hold or give up other leads if you are not employed. If the feel you get for the organization is positive and you are confident you are going to get a firm offer, you must be prepared to ask some key questions.

Employment office interviewers often fail to volunteer information that will answer all the questions important to interviewees. So it is good to have a checklist of your key questions that you can consult if you feel you will get the offer or be a serious candidate for the job.

If the interviewer is relatively new, he or she may not have some of the answers you want, and in a few cases interviewers may give vague or otherwise incomplete answers. If you sense some resistance to your questions, back off for the moment. You will probably get a second interview with the individual who will be your boss if you are hired. He or she will be sure you get the answers you want so you won't be unhappy later.

Interview tips Unless you have enough confidence in your memory to be sure you won't forget important points that you want to make in interviews, write them down in advance. When the time comes, simply take the list out of your pocket or purse. Hold it near your lap so you can glance at it as you talk. Then you won't miss important points. Use a small piece of paper or a 3×5-inch filing card. The following brief example illustrates the idea.

Things I want to mention.

- How I learned about the vacancy through my sister who used to work here and enjoyed it

- Science prize I won in my third year

- My volunteer work as first aid and CPR instructor

- Merit award for employee suggestion when working for Middletown Corporation

- Class I am taking in computer programming

- Dad knows Margaret Jamieson, head of the Finance Department

The items you list will normally be more abbreviated, perhaps only a note for each item.

Arrive early. Plan on getting to your appointment ahead of time because being late can cost you the job. By starting out early, you may be on time even if you run into an unexpected delay. Or you may then be able to phone in and explain why you are delayed.

Show extra courtesy. In many cases, the first person you meet and must deal with when you appear for an interview is a receptionist or a secretary. Be especially courteous and pleasant with this person. Give your name and tell him or her that you have an appointment. Ask the person's name unless you see a nameplate on the desk. If you are invited to have a seat, use the person's name when you are saying thanks. Then when you are seated or have some other opportunity, make a note of the person's name. Names are magic. If you call later or come back in person, your stock will go up if you can address him or her by name. While receptionists and secretaries have no authority to hire you, in a lot of instances they do have some influence. If they have been on the job a long time and are well respected in the organization, it is not unusual for an interviewer to come out after the applicant has gone and ask the receptionist for his or her impressions.

Suppose you were abrupt when you arrived or expressed impatience because you had to wait. When asked, the receptionist might say that you seemed unpleasant or rude. This could be just the remark that tips the scales against you. Make a good impression on everyone, and don't forget to say a friendly word to the receptionist or secretary as you are leaving.

Shake hands as you introduce yourself. The interviewer, man or woman, should rise and offer a handshake to you, whether you are a man or a woman. If an interviewer fails to do this, walk up and offer your hand. Don't hesitate. This is just good manners, and everyone knows it. So establish in the beginning that you know the right thing to do, even if you run into an interviewer who is too bored or too lazy to take the initiative.

Show some enthusiasm. Now that you have come to your big moment, show some personality, some vitality. It would be silly to force yourself to laugh or chuckle. But show some brightness, responsiveness, cordiality. Enthusiasm for the line of work you are in will pay off. If you are applying for a job driving a large tractor-trailer, it would be good to say something like, "Mr. Jones, I've been driving trucks for five years now, and I like every minute of it." Or, "Mrs. Smith, this is exactly what I want. I'm very enthusiastic about it."

Avoid a dull, monotonous tone. Your rehearsals ought to help you with that. Answer questions with a clear, strong, confident voice. It is a serious situation in a sense, but smile once in a while.

Stay agreeable.   Never argue with an interviewer if you want the job. You may not agree with everything interviewers say to you, but remain silent rather than risk an argument. It is proper to correct a statement about your background or qualifications that is factually wrong. For example, if an interviewer should say something like, "I don't think any amount of experience can make up for lack of the right education," don't argue. This is the interviewer's opinion, and your chances of changing it are slim. But the possibility of getting into an argument that could hurt your relationship is substantial.

Suppose, however, an interviewer makes the mistake of saying, "You have a good background but you have no supervisory experience, and it's going to hurt your chances for this job." In fact, you do have a little experience, but it is not evident in the way you described your background. Naturally, you should correct the mistake, saying, for example,

> I realize it isn't made clear in the application, but when I was with the Gallagher Corporation, I trained and supervised new sales representatives for the first two months, until they were given a territory. That was in addition to my regular duties. Also, when I was with the chamber of commerce, I took its six-week course in fundamentals of effective supervision. Would you like me to add explanations of those qualifications to the application?

The interviewer's style.   No two interviewers you meet will be exactly alike. While most are gracious, considerate, and competent, some are clearly in the wrong jobs. You may run into one who has been interviewing for so many years he or she is now bored with it, and the boredom shows. A few just have no class. They handle applicants so routinely their manners border on rudeness. Fortunately, these types are few. Just be mentally prepared to keep your cool. Perform at your best, regardless of whether you like the interviewer or the way he or she acts.

Let the interviewer set the tone and pace and take your cue from that. If you feel a need to, adjust your natural style somewhat. For example, suppose you are naturally talkative, but you find the interviewer is exceptionally quiet and businesslike. In that case it won't help to let your talkativeness have a loose rein. If you are naturally reserved and you get an interviewer who is cheerful and outgoing, try to brighten up somewhat. Compatibility is what you are seeking, and establishing it will be greatly to your advantage.

Be alert and considerate.   Stay alert and sensitive to what is going on around you. Be aware of the interviewer's need to take time out from your discussion. React cooperatively. If you are talking and the phone rings, don't keep on talking. Hesitate to see if the interviewer is going to pick up the phone. Hold back on what you were saying if the interviewer needs to talk. Then don't just sit and listen to the conversation. Look over a copy of your application or resume, review the points you want to cover, or pick up a magazine if it appears the call will last a while.

Don't be an interrupter. We all interrupt once in a while, usually by accident. However, if you keep cutting in, you will be showing a gross lack of tact and consideration. Show that you have learned the importance of consideration.

Use facts to sell yourself.   One of the most delicate problems in being interviewed is to sell the interviewer on the idea that you are a great candidate for the job, without appearing boastful.

The trick is to talk about your accomplishments with facts and avoid offering personal opinions on your fine qualities. An applicant is bragging who says, "My safety record in driving for the Smith Company was really great." The point will go over much better if he or she says: "I drove for the Smith Company over a million miles without an accident or traffic violation."

Similarly, it would be in poor taste for an applicant to boast,

> When I was with the travel agency, I was terrific
> in selling and in getting my customers to rave

about me." Facts are so much better: "When I was with the Elston Travel Agency, I started from scratch. By my third year I was writing two million in business annually. Incidentally, last year six of my customers wrote favorable letters to the owner of the business about the tour plans I worked out for them. I have copies of their letters if you would like to see them, or you can verify this with Mr. Hall, my supervisor there.

Interruptions and probing for negatives

You will be given time to talk and add to your application or resume, but be prepared to be interrupted. With your checklist of important points in hand, it will be easy to get back on track. Try to answer unexpected questions in the same clear, strong, confident, and pleasant voice you were using. Most interviewers will ask questions to probe for negatives. If a question zeroes in on a weakness of yours, give the most favorable answer you can as long as it is based on the truth. Try to stay calm and take time to think over the interviewer's questions and the answer that you think is best.

Of course there may be no good answer. If your scholastic record was abominable and you are asked about how well you did in school, you might show how you are compensating for this weakness: "I regret not taking advantage of the opportunity to learn while I was in school. But the courses I have taken at Harper Community College have helped to fill in some of the gaps."

Asking questions

Interviews should be two-way affairs. Here are some suggestions about questions you should ask and those better avoided. Almost always, there are two interviews involved. The first is often referred to as a screening interview, normally done by a member of the employment office staff, an interviewer. The other is the principal interview. This is normally conducted by the person you will be working for if you are hired. If you don't get all the answers you want in the first interview, you can probably get them from your prospective boss.

You may decide you don't want a second interview. For instance, you may find out from the employment office that the pay is lower than you will accept or that another condition is involved that causes you to lose interest.

Naturally, if you decline the job, you will want to do so pleasantly. If you leave a good impression and part on friendly terms, you have some chance of getting a call later saying your objection has been overcome or the employer has another job to talk with you about.

Accepting an Offer You Like

If you get the offer and like it, here are some points to be sure to settle on:

- For whom will I be working (name and title)?

- How does the job fit into the organization?

- What is the arrangement for uniforms, if needed?

- Is there a cafeteria or restaurants that are nearby, or do most employees bring their lunches with them?

- What does the position pay?

- Is there an employee handbook available that contains information on personnel rules and benefits?

- Is there some literature on the organization's services or products that I could take along?

- Is there a person or office to help arrange car pools?

In addition, if you get to a principal interview with the prospective boss, you may want to ask more about your specific duties and responsibilities.

But don't ask any more questions than necessary. If you like everything you know about the job and you are sure you want it, let some of the less important matters go until you get to work. If you are going to be working in an office, for example, and have seen the women wear dresses or dress slacks, don't ask in the interview if it will be all right if you come to work in jeans.

Avoid sensitive subjects

Wait until later to raise questions about sensitive or delicate subjects. Don't ask them in interview situations unless it is absolutely essential for you to know, and you won't take the job unless you get the answer, whatever the risk.

Some examples of sensitive questions to avoid asking are:

- How soon will I get a vacation?

- When will I get my first raise?

- How long do I have to be here before I can borrow money from the credit union?

- How much sick leave will I be getting?

- How soon will I get paid?

- Will your hospitalization plan pay me if I get pregnant?

- What holidays do I get paid for?

- Am I going to have to work overtime?

- Will I do any traveling?

Uniforms, tools, and deposits

If uniforms are required or if you have to supply certain tools of your own or borrow them by paying a deposit, such subjects ought to be clarified in the interview. Tell the interviewer what you understand the requirement to be and seek confirmation. If you don't have the required deposit, this is the time to speak up. Many employers permit new hires to have such deposits or charges deducted from their first paycheck.

Where uniforms are required, employees are often charged for the first issuance and are responsible for their care and laundering. Two sets are normally provided. When these are worn out, they can be exchanged for new sets at no cost. If they are lost, however, the employee has to buy replacements. In some instances when the charge is in the form of a deposit, after a specified period it is refunded in the case of tools as well as uniforms.

Whether the requirement covers uniforms or tools, the important point is that you need to be sure you can bring the money at the right time or work out some alternative before it is time to begin your new job.

Special and executive benefits

You may be willing to accept a lower salary to start if the organization has a profit-sharing or bonus system that provides extra money. Normally such benefits are explained in the screening interview. An exception is often made in the case of executive bonuses, stock options, or other benefits that may or may not be allocated for managerial positions. Such plans are often secret. Much effort is made to keep a minimum number of managers participating, thus leaving larger slices of the pie to those approved to participate.

If you are applying for a supervisory, managerial, or executive position, be sure to ask specifically if there is a bonus plan. If you don't ask, it is likely you will miss out and learn too late that you are not "on the list," because you were not aware of its existence. Similarly, inquiries ought to be made at the negotiating point about expense account policies, credit cards for phone calls and lunches, club memberships, use of a company car, and other managerial privileges. These discussions are more appropriately held with an officer of the company, who will undoubtedly be giving the principal interview.

Adequate notice for your present employer

When you are told the position is yours if you want it, the question of a starting date may prove difficult to settle on. Many times the hiring organization will want you to come to work immediately. Sometimes you will be replacing a person who left the job suddenly, and you will be pressured to start as soon as the next day.

If this happens, say you will have to talk with your present boss to see what arrangement can be made. In spite of the hardship involved, most new employers will respect your ethics and concern for the organization you are leaving. They will want to think you would give them the same consideration if you were leaving them.

Normally employers give employees two weeks' notice or pay before any layoff. In return, they expect two weeks' notice from employees who quit. You should certainly give the same notice, unless you can reach an agreeable compromise.

If you come to an impasse where the hiring organization says it cannot or will not wait two weeks for you, and the people at the job you are leaving insist on at least two, you will have a tough decision to make. What you do will depend on how badly you want the new job, how well you have been treated by your present employer, and whether you think the hiring organization will hold the job for you.

One possible solution is that you offer a one-week notice and make a strong case to both parties that this is a fair compromise all around. If you have to give up the new opportunity to do the right thing by your present employer, be sure your boss there and others concerned fully realize the sacrifice you made in order not to leave them in a lurch. You could get a very nice surprise, but at the very least you can look for the next opportunity knowing you have put principle above immediate material gain, and that makes you someone very special.

If in the end you decide to leave your present employer with little or no notice, try to help in some way. For example, volunteer to come in evenings and weekends for a short while to keep things above water or to help train your replacement. Do everything possible to avoid leaving any job in bad grace. You may need a good reference from the organization at some time in the future. It is not likely you will get one if you take a "to hell with you and your problems" attitude when you are on your way out. You will observe in time that responsible, fair-but-tough people get a lot of "lucky breaks."

Avoid Negative Reactions

If you are told straight out you are being turned down, in some sense it is a kindness. Being led to believe you have a chance when you really don't is worse. Employment office interviewers and others involved in hiring processes often get into the habit of doing what they consider to be letting unsuccessful applicants down easy. They will say things such as, "Thank you for coming in. You have a good background, and we'll let you know as soon as we can." They know very well you are not what they want and have no intention of calling you. This kind of effort to be "kind" can cause applicants to turn down other offers or bring their job hunting to a stop. They wait in vain for a call that will never come.

Whether you are told you are not to be the chosen one or just have a strong feeling you are not going to get the job, always leave on a cordial, friendly note. The winner may decline, moving you from second to first choice. You can spoil an otherwise fine performance by any show of emotion indicating resentment or annoyance. By taking a turndown gracefully, you at least keep alive the chance you may get a call when a similar vacancy occurs. Every organization has a certain amount of employee turnover. Employees come and go, and job opportunities open time and again in virtually every category. A good exit helps ensure that you will get future consideration.

Make a good exit   How do you make a good exit? If the organization and the job are attractive and exciting as far as you are concerned, say so. All employers like to hire people who are enthusiastic about working for them. When the interview is coming to a close, make a final statement that reflects your sincere interest in the job. If you don't get it, a good closing statement will improve your chances of being called for the next similar vacancy. Extend your hand as you are about to leave, smile, and have something positive ready to say.

Here are some suggestions on what to say as you are leaving with the outcome of your interview in doubt:

> I hope to hear from you soon. I really want this job. You people have a fine reputation, and I'd sure like to be one of you.

> I've certainly enjoyed meeting and talking with you. This is exactly what I've been looking for, and I hope you'll give me a chance to show I can do a great job for you.

> Have I given you everything you need? If there is anything else you want, I'll be glad to supply it right away. I really want this job, and I know you'll like my work.

If you have been definitely turned down and there isn't any doubt that you are out of the running, say something like the following:

> I'm sorry you don't feel I'm just right for the job, but I want to thank you for being honest with me. I'd like to come back later and try again, because I really want to work for your organization. In the meantime, can you give me any suggestions on how I might improve my qualifications so I'll have a better chance when I apply again?

The Follow-Up Call   For any really good job, the employer may have many applicants to consider. Even after getting down to several leading candidates, the decision can be difficult. When it is made, the selected applicant may turn the job down for one reason or another. A follow-up call may help.

When to make the call   Here are some observations about follow-up calls if you are sure you are one of the better candidates:

- About a week after your final session with the last person who interviewed you, call and ask whether the job has been filled. One advantage of doing this is that if the position is filled, you can put it out of your mind and concentrate on other possibilities. If you get an evasive answer, be sensitive to any vibes or hints from the other person's manner. If you get a quick brush-off, there is your answer. The way people react to you almost always means more than the words they say. Tell them thanks and go on with your campaign to find a better job.

- In some cases, when you make this kind of follow-up call, you may get a response that is neither positive nor negative. You might be told that you are still under consideration. However, if you are sure you are a very well-qualified applicant but have not been selected for a week or more after your final interview, you should assume something is wrong. Most jobs urgently need to be filled. If the person you called gives a plausible reason for the delay, perhaps you still have a chance, but don't count on it. Unless you get some positive encouragement, conclude that you are not likely to get the job and concentrate your energies and interests on other opportunities.

- When you make a follow-up call, you may learn immediately you were not selected but that the decision was a close one. Usually in these cases, the person you call will be cordial and perhaps even a bit apologetic. You may learn you were the number two candidate but the other person had more experience or special training that tilted the scales away from you.

These are situations that fully justify your putting some additional time and effort into follow-up actions. Ask whether similar vacancies are anticipated for the near future. Indicate you would like to call once in a while and check out the situation. If you get the "don't call us, we'll call you" routine, you probably don't rate as high as you believe.

If you are invited or encouraged to call once in a while, do it, but don't make a nuisance of yourself. Many possible candidates have had their applications transferred to the "impossibles" file for failure to use common sense.

How often to call is too often? Remember that applications kept on hand get stale. Make your first follow-up call about a month after you learn you definitely lost out to someone else. Then call about every two months thereafter. Or consider dropping by once in a while, even if you just see the receptionist or a secretary and leave a friendly note for the person you have been dealing with. What you are playing for is a first-in-line position if your type of job opens and there is an urgent need to fill it. The percentage of payoff is not very high, but it works often enough to make it worth some time and trouble.

What to say Be sure in making follow-up calls that you come across as a smart, interesting person. It is not smart to call and ask, "Anything for me yet?" or, "I haven't heard from you people, and I was wondering if you had been trying to reach me." Use your own personality and mental or written notes about people you are calling and practice what you are going to say so it comes out smoothly. Here are a few examples:

> Hello, Mr. Martin. This is Jim McClure. I was a candidate for your warehouse foreman job a while back, and you said it would be all right if I check with you occasionally. How are those new forklifts working out?

> Mrs. Martenson? Judy Maxwell. You said it would be okay if I call you once in a while to see if one of your bank teller jobs might be opening up in the near future. We've moved to a new apartment. May I leave my new phone number with you?

> Mr. Brownlow? Jim Hanigan. We talked a while back about a possible spot for me on your marketing team. At the time, you told me someone else had been picked but that I ought to check with you now and then to see if you are expecting

any other openings. I see by the papers you have two major new products coming out in the next few months. If this will mean that more job openings will be coming up, I'd like you to consider me for them.

This is Steve Delaney, Miss Jansen. When we last talked about one of your air freight jobs, you said you thought it would be a good idea if I kept in touch. I really want to be a part of your organization, so I'll be ready anytime something opens up. When I had that interview, you were about to leave on a vacation to the Caribbean Islands. We've always wanted to go there. How was it?

You may prefer to write follow-up notes under these circumstances, but calls are more personal and effective. However, a well-phrased note is better than no follow-up at all. Its main purpose is to remind the individual about your qualifications as well as interest, looking toward future opportunities. Write something along these lines:

I appreciate the time and consideration you gave me in regard to your opening for a sales manager. As you may recall, I'm the person who has been managing sales for the Norton Company for the past five years, during which our volume has gone up more than 500 percent.

I'm still interested and hope you will keep me in mind.

Negotiating an Unacceptable Offer

If the job is offered to you but one or more of the conditions is definitely unacceptable, try some negotiating before you turn the opportunity down. In the event you do decide to negotiate the offer, treat the issue as a problem you are raising because you want to know if the interviewer can solve it. Psychologically and strategically this phrase puts the problem into the laps of the offerers and asks them if they have the ability or authority to solve it. With this approach, you will find most people will want to show you they do have the necessary ability or authority. If they really need you for the job, they will try hard to work things out. If your position is a sound one, you will be surprised how often a settlement is reached.

Don't try to get the offered pay rate hiked up unless you decide that you will not take the job if it doesn't pay more than has been offered. The danger in asking for more money as a bluff is that the employer may conclude you will be dissatisfied with the salary that he or she cannot or will not increase. So the employer will decide not to hire you rather than take the chance you will start hustling your boss for a raise as soon as you get settled in and will quit soon if you don't get it. Leave well enough alone is good advice here.

On the other hand, let's assume you are offered the job but will accept it only if the pay is raised. If you decide to negotiate, understand a few key points about salary structures. Then you will be able to give a logical reason why you should be started above the rate offered most applicants.

Does the existence of standard starting rates mean that no one gets hired at more than the first step of the job's salary range? The answer is a qualified no. There may be as many as six to ten salary range steps for each job in any organization. Most newly hired employees start at the first step and are moved up the scale annually. These within-grade raises reflect accumulated skill and are given in appreciation for continued satisfactory service. Recognizing this, put your request in the light of this rationale by talking convincingly about one or two points that favor your position.

Negotiating for a better salary

You are much better qualified than most applicants. While it is true you cannot know how well qualified the other applicants are, you will know if you have more relevant experience and/or training than most people in your field. If you have been doing the kind of work the prospective job involves for ten or more years, you can probably assume you are better qualified than most applicants. Your extra experience can be a solid reason to give you a better-than-usual rate.

Your negotiating basis can be something like this:

> Ms. Ellsworth, everything about this job is just fine, except the salary. As you have seen, I have more than ten years' experience in this kind of work, and if you check my references you will find that I'm able to do much more than other employees who are newer to this kind of work. I'm afraid I couldn't justify to myself starting at

the figure you mention, so I guess we have a problem. Do you think you can do anything about it?

You have been earning significantly more for the same type of work that is being offered to you. This may or may not be the same as the first reason—that you have more experience than most applicants. If you have included your past and current salary rates on your application, it ought to be evident immediately to the interviewer that the usual starting rate will not be acceptable to you. If the difference is large and the interviewer knows there is absolutely no room to negotiate the salary, you will probably be told you are over-qualified, and you may be.

However, it is almost always possible to make exceptions. At least it is worth a try if you want the job but won't take it unless the salary is raised.

Don't put your salary requirement in the form of a demand or base it on financial need. What you need is not usually relevant; what you deserve is important here. Start by making the point, regardless of the fact that it is evident in your salary history, that the pay offered is significantly less than you have been paid previously for the same type of work.

This is the kind of statement to use in these situations:

Ms. Smith, this is just the kind of job I'm after, but the salary you mentioned is substantially less than I've been paid by other employers. With the experience I've had, I believe you will find I'll be worth much more to you right from the beginning. Also, the rate you mentioned would mean my employment record would show a cut in pay, and it seems to me that would be an unfavorable mark on my record. I don't like to have to bring it up, but we have a problem. Do you think you can do anything about it?

Responding to an Acceptable Offer

When you receive an acceptable offer, you will want to respond immediately. If the offer is made in person or by phone, you can accept right then. You should also follow up with a letter, to confirm.

Worksheet: Common Interview Questions

Here is a list of the most commonly asked interview questions. Prepare for your interview by writing down your responses.

Why did you apply for this job? _____

_____

_____

_____

_____

_____

Why did you choose this career? _____

_____

_____

_____

_____

_____

Why should I hire you? _____

_____

_____

_____

_____

_____

What would you like to tell me about yourself? _____

_____

_____

_____

_____

_____

What are your major strengths? Weaknesses? _____

_____

_____

_____

_____

What did you like best or least about your last job? _____

_____

_____

_____

_____

Why did you leave your last job? _____

_____

_____

_____

_____

How does your education or experience relate to this job? _____

_____

_____

_____

_____

What do you hope to be doing in five years? Ten? _____

_____

_____

_____

_____

What salary do you expect? _____

_____

_____

Worksheet: Strengths and Weaknesses

During your interview, you will probably be asked to describe your strengths. This worksheet will help you develop a list of your strengths so that you are prepared to respond to the interviewer's questions.

Educational Strengths

List any educational qualifications (majors, courses, special training programs) that you have that are relevant to the job for which you are applying.

_____

_____

_____

_____

_____

Job Skill Strengths

List job skills that you have acquired through education or training.

Skill	**Program**
Example: cutting hair	1983 graduate of Phoenix Beauty Academy

List jobs skills you have acquired on the job.

Skill	**Job Responsibility**
Example: managing people	Assistant manager at Designer's Loft Salon

List the most important duties on your most recent job and what skills you need to carry them out.

Duty	**Skill**
Example: keeping supplies in stock	Inventory control

_____   _____

_____   _____

_____   _____

_____   _____

_____   _____

Personal Strengths

Put a check next to each personal trait that is true of you and describe how you used that trait on the job.

_____   1. Punctuality

_____

_____

_____

_____

_____

_____   2. Good Attendance

_____

_____

_____

_____

_____

_____   3. Courtesy/Tact

_____

_____

_____

_____

_____

_____   4. Dedication

_____

_____

_____

_____

_____

_____   5. Initiative

_____   6. Carefulness/Accuracy

_____   7. Productivity

_____   8. Cheerfulness

_____   9. Honesty

_____   10. Loyalty

Weaknesses

One of the best ways to add to your list of strengths is to acknowledge your weaknesses, figure out how to remedy them, and turn them into strengths. List your greatest weaknesses and how you are working to overcome them.

Weakness: _____

Remedy: _____

_____

_____

Weakness: _____

Remedy: _____

_____

_____

Weakness: _____

Remedy: _____

_____

_____

Weakness: _____

Remedy: _____

_____

_____

Weakness: _____

Remedy: _____

_____

_____

Weakness: _____

Remedy: _____

_____

_____

Worksheet: Interview Arrangements

It is essential that you make a good first impression at your interview by being at the right place, at the right time, ready to do your best. Use the following format to get the information you need to have a successful interview.

Company name _____

Street address _____

Travel directions _____

_____

_____

Date and time of interview _____

Name and title of interviewer _____

Room number _____

Names and titles of any others to be at the interview

_____

_____

Person making arrangements _____

Telephone number _____

Materials to bring_____

Company name _____

Street address _____

Travel directions _____

_____

_____

Date and time of interview _____

Name and title of interviewer _____

Room number _____

Names and titles of any others to be at the interview

_____

_____

Person making arrangements _____

Telephone number _____

Materials to bring_____

Worksheet: Questions for Interviewers

The interview is a two-way conversation. You need to gather information to find out if the job you are applying for is really what you want. Here is a list of questions for you to ask the interviewer.

- What might a typical day on this job be like?
- Whom would I report to? May I meet this person?
- Would I supervise anyone? May I meet them?
- Where does this job fit within the company's activities?
- What training programs are offered?
- Are there opportunities for advancement and self-improvement?
- What is the greatest challenge of this position?
- What plans does the company have with regard to . . .? (Mention some development of which you have heard or read.)
- Is the company growing?

Additional questions that may be of importance to you:

- _____
- _____
- _____
- _____
- _____
- _____
- _____
- _____
- _____
- _____
- _____
- _____
- _____
- _____
- _____
- _____

Example: Follow-up Letter

533 Fairview Drive
Orlando, Florida 25177
555-8732
February 20, 19 _____

Ms. Linda Rodriguez
Public Relations Manager
Stevens PR Group
1653 San Rey Boulevard
Orlando, Florida 25175

Dear Ms. Rodriguez:

Thank you for the time you spent with me yesterday and the information about the public relations assistant position you are seeking to fill. As you noted in our discussion, my previous experience and education are directly related to the responsibilities you described.

I remain very interested in working at Stevens PR Group as a public relations assistant and look forward to hearing from you soon.

Sincerely,

Thomas Ross

Worksheet: Follow-up Letter

Draft a follow-up letter for use following interviews that did not result in a job offer, but from which you have reason to believe you may get an offer in the future.

Keep your follow-up letter brief; a handwritten note is acceptable, but get the letter typed if you can. You always gain by making a professional impression.

Thank the addressee for her or his time and courtesy when you were interviewed. Include brief reminders of who you are, how things were left at the close of the interview, and stress your continued interest and availability.

Your Address _____

_____

_____

Telephone: Home _____

Name and Title _____

Organization _____

Department _____

Street _____

City/State/Zip _____

Dear _____:

_____

_____

_____

_____

_____

_____

Sincerely,

_____

Example: Letter Following Rejection

636 Bridge Street
Fort Collins, Colorado 80206
555-1605
April 14, 19 ____

Mr. Michael Costa
Vice President of Sales
Global Manufacturing
245 Fremont Avenue
Denver, Colorado 80226

Dear Mr. Costa:

I enjoyed meeting you last week and appreciated the time you spent with me during my interview. I was disappointed I did not get the sales job, but I thank you for your honesty.

I would really like to work for Global Manufacturing and be a part of its sales team. If you again find a similar position open, I would be grateful for a chance to compete for it.

Sincerely,

Janice O'Keefe

Worksheet: Letter Following Rejection

When someone else gets the job, you will still want to send a follow-up letter.

Thank the interviewer for her or his time, state that you are sorry that an agreement could not be reached, and mention that you would like to be kept in mind for future openings, if this is true.

If it seems appropriate, you can use this letter to mention any special reason why you would like to keep this company in mind—its recent growth in an area you are especially qualified in, for instance.

In the space below, write out a draft of the follow-up letter you will use as a model for cases where you are not the one chosen for the job.

Your Address _____

_____

_____

Telephone: Home _____

Name and Title _____

Organization _____

Department _____

Street _____

City/State/Zip _____

Dear _____:

_____

_____

_____

_____

_____

_____

_____

_____

_____

_____

_____

_____

_____

_____

Sincerely,

_____

Example: Letter of Acceptance

8139 East Kellogg
Topeka, Kansas 66605
January 14, 19_____

Ms. Anne Prioletti
Manager, New Horizons Travel Agency
1118 North Seventh Street
Topeka, Kansas 66611

Dear Ms. Prioletti:

Thank you for calling me yesterday to offer me a position at New Horizons. I am very pleased to accept your offer, and I am confident that my experience in the travel industry will be an asset to the agency.

As we agreed during our last conversation, I will begin on Monday, January 30, at a salary of $1,750 per month. Agency hours are from 10:00 to 6:00, and I am to report for work at 9:30. Please let me know if I have misunderstood any of these arrangements.

Thanks again for your offer. I look forward to working with you at New Horizons Travel Agency.

Sincerely,

Donna Novack

Worksheet: Letter of Acceptance

When as the result of an interview you have been offered a position, it is important to accept formally as well as orally, using your acceptance letter to review important points about the offer and your acceptance as a means of avoiding any possible misunderstandings.

Some important points to be covered include starting date, position title, starting salary, your understanding concerning uniform and tool deposits, and special benefits or arrangements if applicable. Start and finish your letter on a happy, friendly note. Have your letter typed if possible.

Your Address _____

_____

_____

Telephone: Home _____

Name and Title _____

Organization _____

Department _____

Street _____

City/State/Zip _____

Dear _____:

_____

_____

_____

_____

_____

_____

_____

_____

_____

_____

_____

_____

_____

Sincerely,

_____

Promotion in Your Present Job

Better Jobs Where You Are

Most of this book has been concerned with finding a job if you are unemployed or contacting other organizations for a better job if you are already employed.

However, the book ought not end without emphasizing the possibility of getting a better job where you are now working. In a similar vein, if you don't have a job but land one, the advice and information provided in this chapter will help you climb the promotion ladder to better jobs.

Naturally, if you are working in a small organization, such as a retail store, you can't go very far up any ladder. On the other hand, if the organization is fairly large, decide whether you can find what you want in one of its departments.

If the main reason you have been thinking about looking elsewhere has to do with pay, working conditions, hours of work, or workload pressures, don't quit or give notice too soon. Go to your boss and talk it over. If more money is your main desire, you won't usually get anywhere by just asking for a raise. Most managers take pride in feeling they know when and how to take action when a raise is due, and they don't like being told they don't know.

Explain that your need to look elsewhere is because you feel you're ready for more responsibility. If you are a valued employee, your boss will get the point and do whatever can be done to get more money to you in your present job. If it proves impossible, you could find yourself in line for a promotion to a better job in the near future. Whatever the problem, begin by talking it over with your boss before you give notice. However, you may want to shop around and get another job lined up elsewhere before you sit down with the boss to see what can be worked out.

Your boss's reaction will depend to a great extent on whether you have laid the foundations for deserving a better job. If you haven't, start now. You can't build stature overnight. You have to build it one block at a time.

Improve Your Personal Traits

The outcome of whatever discussion you have with your boss is going to be influenced by whether you have built a solid reputation. So if you are employed now, keep trying to improve your personal traits so you become one of the boss's star performers. Then when he or she learns something has to be done to keep you, it will be done, including having a battle with top management for you if necessary.

Naturally, doing more and better work than the other employees is always of prime importance in making yourself valuable. But your personal traits are also extremely important, and one of the most important of these is loyalty. Loyalty is preserved when you take your criticisms to your boss and discuss them in a positive way. Your reputation for loyalty to the boss and the organization can quickly be destroyed if word gets around that you run down the boss. Think carefully about this quotation from the pen of Elbert Hubbard, an early twentieth-century philosopher and writer:

> If you work for an organization, be loyal to it. If you insist on undermining and degrading it, resign your position. Then, when you are on the outside, damn to your heart's content. Otherwise, with the first high wind you will be blown away, and never know why.

A popular pastime with too many employees is badmouthing the boss. Perhaps it is a human trait for people to want to make themselves feel superior by running down others who are in higher organizational positions.

Don't engage in this kind of talk with other employees, however tempting it may be, particularly when the boss has done something to annoy or offend you. It won't do you any more good than complaining to a blank wall, and it can do you a lot of harm. Some workers will join in a session in which employees give vent to their gripes about the boss and then later report to the boss on who said what.

Other important traits merit your attention. The following inventory form will help you identify personal traits. It sets forth the traits or qualities almost all bosses appreciate. Those who rate high on these characteristics get the promotions. They get the boss's best help and support when they need it. Imagine you are a boss. Look at the list of traits from that point of view. Then, if you would like to see how you stand compared to others, rate yourself. Be honest. Whether you are hoping to get a better job where you are now or if you are just out looking for a job, this can be a valuable exercise.

You ought to think carefully about why you gave yourself a rating of less than 5 on any item. When you did, you were indicating you feel you are less than nearly perfect, meaning you need some improvement. You have identified the need. Concentrate on it.

Get More Education or Training

If you are serious about your future, you will learn and prepare yourself for a better job. The greatest boon in this century for people who want to get ahead was the establishment of community colleges.

Traditional colleges are much more expensive. They can be far from home, harder to get into, and oriented principally to the full-time day student. Community colleges are none of these.

They not only offer a great many courses at night and on Saturdays, they are also less academic and more attuned to the job-related needs of working adults.

Many people cannot get a better job because they are undereducated or because they are on or near the top rung of their career ladders. The only practical ways for them to get ahead are to prepare for a management job or shift onto a different career ladder.

Most community colleges offer courses in management and supervision, accounting, business administration, engineering, merchandising, computer programming, electrical work, heating and air conditioning, and preparation for other fields that also offer good futures.

Take as many courses as you can. Take only one at a time if that is all you can afford.

If you do take part-time college work or training at other institutions, make the most of it by getting your boss involved. Ask him or her for an opinion on what you plan to do. Report experiences and progress now and then. This is bound to make a favorable impression and help your cause in trying to get a better job where you are now employed.

Ask that a copy of your completion paper or certificate be placed in your personnel file.

Seek Help from Your Boss

If there is clearly no further opportunity for you in your department, see if your boss will help you get a better spot elsewhere in the organization. Try to arrange a talk about it in some private place. Perhaps you can have lunch together or have a cup of coffee at the snack bar at a table for two. Open the conversation by talking about your job in a positive way. This sets a better tone for your request than by starting off with complaints. Don't overdo it. What you say will depend on your circumstances, but this is the general idea:

> Ms. Stevens, I've been working for you for about three years now, and I want to say I've enjoyed it. I like the work, and I think the organization is great. But I have a problem. . . .

State your problem or need simply

Suppose that getting more money is the main problem. Spend a few minutes reviewing the history of your salary over the time you have been with the organization. Then explain why you need to look elsewhere for greater chances for advancement. Don't ask for a raise.

> My problem, frankly, is that I believe I'm ready to take on more responsibility. At this time, I'm not asking for a raise, but I've had only two increases since I've been here, and the last one was more than a year ago. For several reasons, I

have to find a way to grow, careerwise. What it adds up to is I have to go where there are more opportunities for advancement. I like this organization, and I'd like to stay. Would you help me get something in one of the other departments that would carry a higher salary range? I plan to go to night school to improve my qualifications, but I first would like to see where I am going to land.

By taking this kind of approach, you indicate indirectly that you would like a raise in pay, but you avoid putting your boss on the spot. If you are a valued employee, the hint might get you a raise, if that is what you would be satisfied with. However, a better job should mean one with better opportunities to move up to more responsibility as well as more pay.

Request something specific

Presumably you want help in getting transferred to another department where you will be on a new and expanded career ladder. If your boss indicates a willingness to see what can be done, try to get agreement that he or she will do something more specific. For example, a call to the personnel office asking its cooperation in helping you get reassigned could be useful to you. If you have in mind some particular section or department where you would like to be, see if your boss knows the top person there and would be willing to help you get an appointment to talk about future possibilities.

Your boss may not give you any help. But because you plan to start looking around yourself and are determined to make a change anyway, you will not have lost anything by asking.

Seek Cooperation from the Personnel Staff

If your boss takes the initiative and helps you land a better job quickly in some other part of the organization, fine. But if you get only promises without action, you will need to start out on your own, provided you are confident your boss will give you a favorable recommendation. The first place to start is the personnel or employment office. The authority most personnel offices have is limited. They are service groups, which means with rare exceptions they can only make recommendations. Nevertheless, after clearing with your boss what you are about to do, ask for an appointment with the top person in the personnel organization. Don't start with an interviewer. Try to see the personnel director, or at least the employment manager, first. It is best if the interviewers get the word from one of the top people that they should help you get a good reassignment. Things will go even better for you if your boss makes your appointment with the top person.

Stress wanting more responsibility

When you see the personnel chief, go overboard on being cheerful and confident. Begin by emphasizing how much you enjoy working for the organization. Stress the point that you want to exhaust all possibilities there before you start looking elsewhere. The first question you will likely be asked is, "Why?" You may have more than one reason for wanting to get out of your present job. Pick the one you think is least likely to cause an unfavorable reaction and stick to it. Instead of saying there is no opportunity to get ahead, say you want to be where there are more opportunities to take on responsibility. Perhaps another department has a good training program that helps employees qualify for promotions.

Don't stress wanting more money

Mention it. Instead of complaining your present job doesn't pay enough, make the point that you are ready for a more challenging assignment. You don't need to talk directly about more money in most of these situations. You are after an assignment with more responsibility, which means more pay. And don't say you are bored with your present job. Say you feel you have outgrown it. If you can't stand your boss or don't get along well with some of the other employees, don't mention those problems at all.

Realistically, it is not likely the personnel manager will directly seek a transfer for you into a better job. Expect to get passed along to an interviewer or some placement specialist. Only if the organization is expanding rapidly can you expect much action on the part of the interviewer or other specialist. It is important to touch base with him or her, but you are probably going to have to start making some moves on your own.

Getting Appointments with Other Bosses

If you have been working in a relatively small- to medium-sized organization for a few years, the chances are good you already know what other departments do. You should also be acquainted with some of the other bosses and employees who work in other sections. Get to meet the heads of other sections and departments by using some ingenuity and persistence. If one of them wants you for a good job, the transfer will be processed by the personnel office. But the final say will ordinarily be with your new boss.

In general, managers or executives who hold the most important jobs are the least accessible. You will almost always need an appointment to get to see them. This is where friends can come in handy. Friends are often instrumental in helping land good jobs. What is more, in most cases, they enjoy doing it. An old adage says, "to accept a favor from a friend is to confer one." So make as many friends in the organization as you can, in all departments and sections. Introduce yourself to other employees when suitable occasions arise. It takes a while to convert acquaintances into friends. Friends within the organization can introduce you to their bosses and can tip you off when they learn a job is about to open up where they work.

Try through the secretary

Secretaries are important because they can help you get the appointments that you want. If you don't have friends in the right places and you need to meet target people on your own, begin by making up a list of the names, titles, and room and phone numbers. Don't phone first. Stop by and meet the individual's secretary or assistant. Secretaries will not only get your name and phone number, but they will also ask about your reason for wanting to have an appointment.

Next, leave a personal note

Very few secretaries can make an appointment for you. The best they can do is convey your request to their bosses and then let you know whether you will be seen. Ask them if they will please give their boss a message for you. Have your message written out in advance, addressed to the individual you want to see and use courtesy titles. In the note, don't request an interview for a possible job opening. To do so will invite a turndown if no current vacancy exists suitable for you. What you need is an opportunity to get to meet and know your target and to have a chance to impress the individual so favorably you will get a call when the first appropriate vacancy is anticipated. Your note can read something along these lines:

Mr. Gomez:

I work for Mr. Moore in the customer service section and have been there about three years now. I enjoy it, but the section is small, and I am at a dead-end there in terms of my career. I understand there are jobs in your department that can use people with my background. While I realize that you may not have a suitable opening at present, would you give me a few minutes so that I can meet you and tell you more about my interests? The phone number in our section where your secretary can reach me is extension 6107. My boss has given his approval for my request and will be glad to talk with you about my work.

The art of gentle persistence

Rather than try to explain to the secretary or assistant the purpose of your request for an appointment, just hand over the note and wait as it is read. Then ask, "Will you please see that Mr. Gomez gets it and let me know if he will see me?" Again, you are not asking the other person to make an appointment for you. You are only asking that he or she pass your note along. At this point you may be asked to leave a resume or a copy of the organization's employment application. Don't bring one. A resume is just a cold, impersonal piece of paper. If you hand one over at this point, the secretary will show it to the boss. The possibility is great that the busy executive will glance at it and tell the secretary to call you and say it will be kept on file. You will have struck out without even getting to bat. On the other hand, if you get to meet the person and sell yourself, the outcome might be entirely different. Call the secretary after several days and inquire if there has been an opportunity to hand over your note. If the boss hasn't gotten it yet, you will have given the secretary the first reminder. If then you don't get a call or explanation in another week, stop by personally and try to find out what the problem is. Be persistent if need be, but gently persistent—that is the key phrase.

If it is a place where you would really like to work and you are sure there are good jobs there for which you are reasonably well qualified, don't give up. It is probably time for an end run.

Seeing other bosses without appointments

In using your ingenuity to get to meet executives you have not been able to see by going through normal channels, you need to know your target. Friends and your boss may be able to point out the person in the cafeteria, parking lot, hallways. After you are sure you know your target by sight, come in at least 20 minutes early a few mornings and try to intercept her or him before the day's business starts. Or wait until after the close of official hours. Many secretaries leave the building exactly at closing time. Managers often stay later and are left "unguarded." Take advantage of these openings. Know what you plan to say and how you want to say it.

You may have only one chance. So when you meet your target, you will need to turn in an exceptionally good performance. You will probably be facing several hurdles. First, most likely no suitable opening for you exists at the moment. You may be getting only a courtesy meeting, granted because you are an employee of the organization or because he or she knows your boss and wants to be cooperative. And if you had to use some tactic to present yourself directly, there could be some resentment. Nevertheless, it is extremely important not to approach the person with a grim life-or-death attitude. Smiles are infectious. Use your most pleasant, relaxed manner. Your first need is to be liked as a person. Qualifications can come later. If you have sprung out of nowhere and caught the person unexpectedly, put on a big grin and introduce yourself. State your business in a way that makes it hard for the individual to respond with a quick or definite no.

This is the idea:

> Good morning, Mrs. Smith, I'm Joan Barber from the data entry section. May I have a few minutes of your time? My boss, Mr. Marshall, thought I ought to meet you and see if you would keep me in mind the next time you have an opening for a programmer trainee. I understand you sometimes take on people with qualifications similar to mine. May I tell you something about myself?

Don't offer a resume　You may have barged in at a bad time, when the person is working on a priority deadline or hurrying somewhere and just can't spend any time with you. You have no right to feel resentful because you did arrive unexpectedly, but you will almost always be offered an appointment to come back later or be told to see the secretary and arrange one. At this first meeting, don't hand over a resume or application. That can end things quickly if your qualifications are weak. Then it will be even more important for you to sell yourself on the basis of your ambition and personal traits.

Also, if you hold off until you have a chance to learn more about the job, you will have a good chance to tailor your resume somewhat to fit the position. In doing so, you will emphasize whatever parts of your background are most applicable to the job you would like to land.

When you get the meeting you want, much of what has been suggested in Chapter 6 applies. However, one item will probably come in for more intensive questioning now—the reason you want a change. The individual you are meeting may even suspect that because your boss is helping you get a job in another section, he or she may be unloading someone whose performance is not very good. The most acceptable reasons are based on ambition. They include wanting more challenging work or getting out of a dead-end job with few opportunities for moving up to greater responsibility.

If there happens to be an immediate opening you are to be considered for, or if you get some definite encouragement about future possibilities, invite the person to call and talk with your boss about your performance and attitude. You can rely on the fact that such a call is going to be made anyway before any papers are processed for your transfer. Your suggesting it will bolster the other person's confidence that you will be an asset in the new job.

Then as soon as you get back to your regular job, tell your boss what happened. See if he or she will call, giving you a good recommendation and indicating a willingness to release you with reasonable advance notice.

The follow-up note No matter what the result, write a brief follow-up note expressing your thanks for the meeting and indicating your continuing interest. A short note will do, something like this:

> Mr. Ogata:
> Thanks very much for talking with me about a possible career opportunity in your section. I'm very enthusiastic about the possibility of going to work for you when you have an opening you feel is suitable.

Or, another example:

> Mrs. Warner:
> Thanks very much for talking with me about a possible career opportunity in your section. I'm

sorry you don't feel my qualifications fit the kinds of jobs you have now, but if you change your mind, I believe you will find I am a fast learner and a very hard worker. I plan to enroll in some night courses next month and will be taking accounting and finance, which you said are important for people coming into your department.

Instead of putting your note into the organization's mail system, take it personally to the individual's secretary, using the note as another opportunity to build your friendship. A secretary who likes you, in such a situation, can remind the boss about your interests when a suitable job is opening up.

Moving Up to the Boss's Job

No discussion of getting a better job within your organization would be complete without some points about taking over your boss's job when he or she leaves it. Bosses, as all employees, come and go. But most of all, they get promoted. In a typical large organization a chain of command may involve as many as a half-dozen executive and supervisory positions. In many instances, when one of the top jobs opens up, a whole chain of promotions results. Each manager gets bumped up to her or his boss's position. At the middle to higher levels, there isn't much competition. Often not more than two or three people are given consideration. Only if none of those is deemed sufficiently experienced or competent is an outsider brought in and given the job. However, a big scramble often occurs at the first supervisory level. Here the span of control can be a dozen or more. Some of them are good candidates for the promotion.

If you want to be the successful candidate when the time comes, you need to start preparing the groundwork well in advance. You need to become one of the favorite people with two individuals—your boss and your boss's boss. When your boss's job is about to open up, he or she will often have the most to say about who first deserves the job. There are exceptions. For instance, if your boss is being fired or is quitting under fire, her or his recommendation may not mean much and might even be the kiss of death. Nevertheless, in most cases a recommendation from your boss will be invaluable.

Become well liked

To be sure your boss will give you that recommendation, become the one on the staff who is most admired and most valued. Get yourself as far ahead of your competitors as you possibly can. Become outstanding in these four ways: (1) doing your work better and faster than the others, or at least as well and quickly as you can; (2) rating higher in your boss's estimation on these important personal traits: punctuality, attendance, courtesy, dedication, initiative, carefulness, productivity, cheerfulness, honesty, and, last but far from least, loyalty; (3) establishing a friendship with your boss; and (4) getting to know and be known by your boss's boss.

Establishing a friendship with your boss does not mean you should try to socialize or make an effort to become chummy. It is considered poor management policy, and with good reason, for bosses to fraternize with employees. There is too much risk of on-the-job favoritism. This will be resented, justifiably, by other employees. And, if it is a male/female situation, tongues will wag, resulting in jeopardy to future career opportunities.

Establish the right kind of friendship with the boss by being cheerful and inquiring about her or his family and leisure interests, such as hobbies, arts, or sports. Be cooperative in all things and show supportive leadership. If the boss initiates a new policy or procedure, get fully behind it and help make it work. If more employee suggestions are called for, put your brain to work and come up with some good ones. If a charity drive is conducted, offer to help with it and give what you can afford.

Show leadership qualities

When an employee in your unit has a special event, be the first to form a small committee. Have one person take up the collection, let another buy the present, and a third go out and select a card. Wrap the present yourself and ask the boss to add an appropriate message. Have everyone sign the card and arrange a presentation ceremony. You are showing your leadership qualities. Once in a while, have a cup of coffee with your boss or, better, ask her or him if you can go to lunch together. Then offer a suggestion about how the work can be done faster, better, or cheaper. The idea may have flaws and never get off the ground. What is important is the supportive, positive attitude you are showing. But don't overdo it. You may think that you don't care whether the boss thinks that you are "apple polishing" or if the other employees resent what you are doing. However, it can matter. So be discreet, sincere, and restrained in your friendly, supportive relationship with the boss. But keep working at it—quietly but steadily.

Get to be liked by your boss's boss

You need to make sure your boss's boss knows who you are and has favorable impressions of you before the time comes when you want to be considered for moving up the ladder. This requires good thinking, finesse, and alertness. In the first place, many bosses like to keep a shield between supervisors and their employees. Second, you need to accomplish your objectives without annoying your boss. These concerns should make you aware you need to be skillful in what you do. This involves the very real world of office politics. There is nothing wrong with participating if you are long on tact and have a good sense of timing.

The best way to get favorable attention from your boss's boss is to do your work in an outstanding manner. You are bound to be mentioned now and then with enthusiasm by the person for whom you are doing such a good job. Also, your boss probably talks occasionally with his or her boss about each employee, such as at performance rating time. Next, be alert for opportunities to talk with the "higher-ups" in the organization. Your boss may go on business trips. Sometimes an acting supervisor will be appointed, but as often as not the boss's boss will take charge.

These can be important opportunities for you; make the most of them. Strive to be cheerful, confident, and 110 percent responsive. No matter what the boss's boss asks for, deliver it in world record time, but double-check and triple-check it for accuracy.

Give more than the minimum in time and effort

Stay overtime if necessary, even if it is not authorized. Work Saturdays and Sundays, with no extra pay if need be, in order to make a big and lasting impression. You can make favorable impressions that will stand you in good stead.

To summarize briefly, if you are employed and you like the place but want a better job, get the inside track on your boss's job. It may open sooner than you think. Perform extra well, maintain desirable personal traits, show leadership qualities in many little ways. Establish friendly relations with your boss and your boss's boss. These are real ways to promotion and pay, but not the only ways. Let's consider some others that are also very important.

Many organizations offer in-service courses in supervisory and management principles and methods. If your organization does, try to enroll. You should start with courses designed for "first line" supervisors if you have no prior training or experience. They are usually the most helpful and least theoretical courses. They would also be the most suitable for you in terms of eligibility if you are not yet in a supervisory capacity. If you already are, you will want to consider the more advanced programs. If none is offered by your organization, get into such courses offered by local colleges, universities, or management training companies. Don't be modest if you enroll, particularly if you are spending your own time and money on this kind of self-improvement. Ask your boss and his or her boss for advice on which courses to take. Talk frequently about what you are learning when opportunities present themselves within your organization. And be sure a note is entered in your personnel file when you have completed such courses.

Worksheet: Personal Traits Inventory

Rating Scale

5-Near perfect	2-A little weak
4-Unusually good	1-Not good at all
3-About average	0-A real problem

Important Qualities

1. **Punctuality**—getting to work on time, even in very bad weather, when almost everyone else is late. □

2. **Attendance**—being on the job just about every day, coming to work even when not feeling so hot; good health. □

3. **Courtesy/Tact**—maintaining friendly relationships with other employees, suppliers, customers, and others. □

4. **Dedication**—willingness to do more than required, to show a sincere interest in the organization's success. □

5. **Initiative**—the ability to do the right thing at the right time, without having to be told. □

6. **Carefulness/Accuracy**—thinking about the work, and doing it with few if any errors. □

7. **Productivity**—the ability to work fast while doing high-quality, accurate work. □

8. **Cheerfulness**—acting pleasant and optimistic even in the face of problems, difficulties, or obstacles. □

9. **Honesty**—being truthful, and never taking anything for yourself that belongs to the organization, without permission. □

10. **Loyalty**—avoiding behind-the-back criticism of the boss or the organization. □

Worksheet: Building Toward a Better Job Where You Are Presently Employed

If you are working for a medium-to-large organization and wish to try to land a better job in some other section or department, use this format to develop a list of supervisors and executives to approach.

Name/title of job target _____

Name of supervisor/manager _____

Location/phone _____

Name of secretary _____

Action taken, date _____

Results, next step _____

_____

_____

_____

Name/title of job target _____

Name of supervisor/manager _____

Location/phone _____

Name of secretary _____

Action taken, date _____

Results, next step _____

_____

_____

_____

Name/title of job target _____

Name of supervisor/manager _____

Location/phone _____

Name of secretary _____

Action taken, date _____

Results, next step _____

_____

_____

_____

VGM CAREER BOOKS

CAREER DIRECTORIES
Careers Encyclopedia
Dictionary of Occupational Titles
Occupational Outlook Handbook

CAREERS FOR
Animal Lovers
Bookworms
Computer Buffs
Crafty People
Culture Lovers
Environmental Types
Film Buffs
Foreign Language Aficionados
Good Samaritans
Gourmets
History Buffs
Kids at Heart
Nature Lovers
Number Crunchers
Sports Nuts
Travel Buffs

CAREERS IN
Accounting; Advertising; Business; Child
Care; Communications; Computers;
Education; Engineering; Finance;
Government; Health Care; High Tech;
Law; Marketing; Medicine; Science;
Social & Rehabilitation Services

CAREER PLANNING
Beginning Entrepreneur
Career Planning & Development for
    College Students & Recent Graduates
Careers Checklists
Cover Letters They Don't Forget
Executive Job Search Strategies
Guide to Basic Resume Writing
Joyce Lain Kennedy's Career Book
Slam Dunk Resumes
Successful Interviewing for College
    Seniors

HOW TO
Approach an Advertising Agency and
    Walk Away with the Job You Want
Bounce Back Quickly After
    Losing Your Job
Change Your Career
Choose the Right Career
Get & Keep Your First Job
Get into the Right Law School
Get People to Do Things
    Your Way
Have a Winning Job Interview
Jump Start a Stalled Career
Land a Better Job
Launch Your Career in TV News
Make the Right Career Moves
Market Your College Degree
Move from College into a
    Secure Job
Negotiate the Raise
    You Deserve
Prepare a *Curriculum Vitae*
Prepare for College
Run Your Own Home Business
Succeed in College
Succeed in High School
Write Successful Cover Letters
Write a Winning Resume
Write Your College
    Application Essay

OPPORTUNITIES IN
Accounting
Acting
Advertising

Aerospace
Agriculture
Airline
Animal & Pet Care
Architecture
Automotive Service
Banking
Beauty Culture
Biological Sciences
Biotechnology
Book Publishing
Broadcasting
Building Construction Trades
Business Communication
Business Management
Cable Television
CAD/CAM
Carpentry
Chemistry
Child Care
Chiropractic
Civil Engineering
Cleaning Service
Commercial Art & Graphic Design
Computer Maintenance
Computer Science
Counseling & Development
Crafts
Culinary
Customer Service
Data Processing
Dental Care
Desktop Publishing
Direct Marketing
Drafting
Electrical Trades
Electronic & Electrical Engineering
Electronics
Energy
Engineering
Engineering Technology
Environmental
Eye Care
Fashion
Fast Food
Federal Government
Film
Financial
Fire Protection Services
Fitness
Food Services
Foreign Language
Forestry
Government Service
Health & Medical
High Tech
Home Economics
Homecare Services
Hospital Administration
Hotel & Motel Management
Human Resource Management
Information Systems
Installation & Repair
Insurance
Interior Design
International Business
Journalism
Laser Technology
Law
Law Enforcement & Criminal
    Justice
Library & Information Science
Machine Trades
Magazine Publishing
Marine & Maritime
Masonry
Marketing
Materials Science
Mechanical Engineering
Medical Imaging
Medical Technology

Metalworking
Military
Modeling
Music
Newspaper Publishing
Nonprofit Organizations
Nursing
Nutrition
Occupational Therapy
Office Occupations
Packaging Science
Paralegal
Paramedical
Part-time & Summer Jobs
Performing Arts
Petroleum
Pharmacy
Photography
Physical Therapy
Physician
Plastics
Plumbing & Pipe Fitting
Postal Service
Printing
Property Management
Psychology
Public Health
Public Relations
Purchasing
Real Estate
Recreation & Leisure
Refrigeration & Air Conditioning
Religious Service
Restaurant
Retailing
Robotics
Sales
Secretarial
Securities
Social Science
Social Work
Speech-Language Pathology
Sports & Athletics
Sports Medicine
State & Local Government
Teaching
Technical Writing &
    Communications
Telecommunications
Telemarketing
Television & Video
Theatrical Design & Production
Tool & Die
Transportation
Travel
Trucking
Veterinary Medicine
Visual Arts
Vocational & Technical
Warehousing
Waste Management
Welding
Word Processing
Writing
Your Own Service Business

RESUMES FOR
Advertising Careers
Banking and Financial Careers
College Students &
    Recent Graduates
Communications Careers
Education Careers
Engineering Careers
Environmental Careers
Health and Medical Careers
High School Graduates
High Tech Careers
Midcareer Job Changes
Sales and Marketing Careers
Scientific and Technical Careers

VGM Career Horizons
a division of NTC *Publishing Group*
4255 West Touhy Avenue
Lincolnwood, Illinois 60646-1975